Armed Forces of the World

edited by
Robert C. Sellers

The Praeger Special Studies program—utilizing the most modern and efficient book production techniques and a selective worldwide distribution network—makes available to the academic, government, and business communities significant, timely research in U.S. and international economic, social, and political development.

Armed Forces of the World
A Reference Handbook
FOURTH EDITION

PRAEGER SPECIAL STUDIES IN INTERNATIONAL POLITICS AND GOVERNMENT

Praeger Publishers New York London

UA15
.R43
    The Reference handbook of the armed forces of the world
      1966–
    Washington, Robert C. Sellers & Associates.

      v. 24cm. annual.

    1. Armed Forces.   I. Sellers (Robert C.) & Associates, Washington.   II. Title: Armed forces of the world

UA15. R43   66-17547

Library of Congress   [1]

PRAEGER PUBLISHERS
200 Park Avenue, New York, N.Y. 10017, U.S.A.

Published in the United States of America in 1977
by Praeger Publishers, Inc.
789 038 987654321
All rights reserved

© 1971, 1977 by Robert C. Sellers

Printed in the United States of America

PREFACE

Worldwide response to the three earlier editions of <u>Armed Forces of the World: A Reference Handbook</u> has been such as to confirm the need for a book that presents military posture data in ready-reference format. As such, it will be revised periodically.

Figures used throughout the book are arrived at by surveys to the governments concerned and a literature search in military and political journals from all over the world. The data is as accurate as is humanly possible under the security restrictions of each country.

As each edition is produced, attempts will be made to include new areas of data and information, such as this edition does by including National Flag, Official Language, and Combat Effectiveness evaluation. The editor welcomes feedback that may suggest how future editions may be improved.

A number of most significant highlights can be ascertained from this new edition of <u>Armed Forces of the World</u>:

- Approximately $300-billion is now being expended annually to support the armed forces of all nations.
- Approximately 22 million men and women are in the armed forces of the world.
- Approximately $70-billion is being expended annually on new weapons procurements.
- Nine of the nations of the world account for 98% of all arms sales:

United States	49.0%
Soviet Union	30.0%
France	5.0%
China	3.5%
United Kingdom	3.2%
Czechoslovakia	2.0%
Poland	1.9%
West Germany	1.9%
Canada	1.8%

- The most significant purchases have been made by the Arab States in the Middle East--a total of over $15-billion since 1973.

Although national security is the first mandate of any government, it is ironic to consider the above and align it with the fact that all governments, all private institutions throughout the world spend less than an estimated $75-million per year on arms control and disarmament efforts.

EXPLANATION OF HEADINGS

Defense Budget
    Annual budget appropriated by Government concerned.
Population
    Total population of nation concerned.
Manpower in the Armed Forces
    Total manpower in armed forces.
Defense as % of GNP
    Percentage of Gross National Product allocated for defense.

ARMY

MANPOWER
    Total regular forces.
GENERAL
    General organizational structure.
PRINCIPAL EQUIPMENT
    General equipment with emphasis on other than conventional light hand-carried arms, if in inventory.

NAVY

MANPOWER
    Total regular forces.
GENERAL
    General comments on fleet.
PRINCIPAL EQUIPMENT
    Quantity and Type of Vessels comprising fleet.
    Quantity and Type of Aircraft comprising naval aviation element.

AIR FORCE

MANPOWER
    Total regular forces.
GENERAL
    General comments on force.
PRINCIPAL EQUIPMENT
    Quantity and Type of Aircraft comprising force. Quantity and Type of Missiles in use.

MISCELLANEOUS DATA

DEFENSE AGREEMENTS
    Treaties and/or alliances.
MAP TYPE ASSISTANCE RECEIVED FROM
    Source of military assistance.
INTERNAL SECURITY FORCES
    Internal Security or Police Forces represent in most countries an extension of military capability; as such they are given for any country wherein they are organized as an arm of the national government.
CONSCRIPTION LAWS
    Details of conscription laws and terms of service.
MILITARY SCHOOLS
    Self-explanatory.
NATIONAL FLAG & OFFICIAL LANGUAGE - Self explanatory.
COMBAT EFFECTIVENESS
    An assessment related to two classes: (1) in relation to bordering states; (2) in relation to East/West power blocs.

Armed Forces of the World

AFGHANISTAN

Defense Budget	$ 45,000,000
Population	18,000,000
Manpower in the Armed Forces	88,000
Defense as % of GNP	3%

ARMY

MANPOWER
　　80,000 men (Reserves of 200,000)

GENERAL
　　The Ministry of National Defense involves chiefly the Army under whose jurisdiction the Air Force operates. Combat units are three tactical corps and four separate divisions. Corps headquarters at Kabul, Gardez and Kandahar control divisional units within assigned territorial areas. There is one brigade of elite Palace Guards.

PRINCIPAL EQUIPMENT
　　Weapons:　　250　T-54 Tanks
　　　　　　　　 200　T-34 Tanks
　　　　　　　　　70　PT-76 Tanks
　　　　　　　　300+ Armored Cars
　　　　　　　　500　Artillery Pieces
　　Missiles:　 Guideline SAM
　　　　　　　 Snapper

NAVY

MANPOWER
　　As a landlocked nation, Afghanistan has no Navy.

AIR FORCE

MANPOWER
　　8,000 men (Reserves of 12,000)

GENERAL
　　Currently operating with combat strength of about 200 aircraft.

PRINCIPAL EQUIPMENT
　　Aircraft:　Fighter-Bombers　　70 MiG-17s
　　　　　　　Light-Bombers　　　 20 Il-28s
　　　　　　　　　　　　　　　　　 30 Su-7s
　　　　　　　Interceptors　　　　40 MiG-21s
　　　　　　　　　　　　　　　　　 12 MiG-19s
　　　　　　　Transports　　　　　25 Il-14s
　　　　　　　　　　　　　　　　　 3 Il-18s
　　　　　　　　　　　　　　　　　 10 An-2s
　　　　　　　Helicopters　　　　 18 Mi-4s
　　　　　　　　　　　　　　　　　 2 Mi-8s
　　　　　　　Trainers　　　　　　Yak-11
　　　　　　　　　　　　　　　　　 Yak-18
　　　　　　　　　　　　　　　　　 MiG-15 UTI

Missiles: Guideline SAM
Atoll AAM

BASES
Bagram, Kabul, Shindand, Mazar-i-Sharif, Kandahar, Sherpur, Kundiz

MISCELLANEOUS DATA

DEFENSE AGREEMENTS
Treaty of Neutrality and Non-Aggression with USSR, running until Aug. 6, 1975.

MAP TYPE ASSISTANCE RECEIVED FROM
Czechoslovakia, USSR, U.S.

INTERNAL SECURITY FORCES
Gendarmerie of 21,000 men.

CONSCRIPTION LAW
Selective conscription with 2 years service with Reserve liability up to age 42.

MILITARY SCHOOLS
Royal Afghan Military Academy, The Military School (preparatory), Noncommissioned Officer's School.

NATIONAL FLAG
Black, red, green (vertical) with a white symbol in the center.

OFFICIAL LANGUAGE
Pushtu, called the national language in the Constitution, and Dari (Persian).

COMBAT EFFECTIVENESS
Excellent

SPECIAL NOTES
Numerous officers have been trained overseas in U.S., Turkey, and USSR. In recent years, most are sent to the USSR.

Because of extensive military assistance from the USSR, the armed forces are almost completely dependent upon the Soviets not only for equipment, but also for logistic support.

The country has its own ordnance plant for the production of light arms and ammunition.

Country has $600-million Soviet loan for development purposes as of January 1975.

The Soviets have constructed a three-lane highway through Afghanistan leading from Soviet Central Asia to the northern frontier of Pakistan.

ALBANIA

Defense Budget	$120,000,000
Population	2,135,600
Manpower in the Armed Forces	43,000
Defense as % of GNP	13%

DEFENSE ESTABLISHMENT

The armed forces are under the Ministry of People's Defense, and all elements are included within the People's Army .. this encompasses the ground, naval and air arms.

ARMY

MANPOWER
   35,000 men

GENERAL

The People's Army, encompasses the ground, naval and air arms of the regular armed forces, under the Ministry of People's Defense.

Total ground force strength is equivalent to two divisions - and the brigade is used as the basic tactical unit with about three thousand men each. There is 1 tank and five infantry brigades.

Infantry brigades contain 3 infantry battalions and a lightly equipped artillery regiment.

Mobilization potential is available in age group 15 to 50 ... about 375,000 men.

PRINCIPAL EQUIPMENT

   Weapons: 100+ T-34 Tanks
              15   T-54 Tanks
              5   T-59 Tanks
              5   T-62 Tanks
              Light and Heavy Artillery
              200+ Armored Cars
   Missiles: Guideline SAM

NAVY

MANPOWER
   3,000 men

GENERAL

Naval units are subordinate to the Coastal Defense Command and are sub-divided into three commands: Submarine and Vlore Sea Defense Brigade, and the Durres Sea Defense Brigade.

PRINCIPAL EQUIPMENT

   Ships: 4 Submarines
              8 Minesweepers
              1 Submarine Support Ship
              1 Degaussing Ship
              40 MTB and Coastal Patrol Craft
              6 Hydrofoil Vessels
   Missiles: Coastal Defense SSMs

AIR FORCE

MANPOWER
    5,000 men

GENERAL
    Air defense artillery and missile units are included with the air force and account for about two-thirds of its personnel strength.

PRINCIPAL EQUIPMENT

<u>Aircraft</u>:   Fighter-Bombers   24 MiG-15s
                                      35 MiG-17s
                                      12 MiG-19s
                                      20 MiG-21s
              Transports   2 Li-2s
                                      3 Il-14s
                                      10 An-2s
              Helicopters   10 Mi-1s
                                      10 Mi-4s

<u>Missiles</u>:   Guideline SAM
              Atoll SAM

MISCELLANEOUS DATA

DEFENSE AGREEMENTS
    Originally member of Warsaw Pact, but withdrew in protest against Soviet invasion of Czechoslovakia.

MAP TYPE ASSISTANCE RECEIVED FROM
    USSR, Red China

INTERNAL SECURITY FORCES
    15,000 para-military force
    12,500 in Directorate of State Security, The People's Police, and Frontier Guards.

CONSCRIPTION LAW
    Men 19 to 35 are liable for 2 years' service in Army; 3 years in Navy and Air Force. All males from 35 to 55 are subject to Reserve Duty.

MILITARY SCHOOLS
    Skanderbeg Military School (preparatory), Enver Hoxha United Army Officer's School, Mehmet Shehu Military Academy (advanced).

NATIONAL FLAG
    Red, with a black double-headed eagle and a red, gold-edged 5-pointed star above it.

OFFICIAL LANGUAGE
    Gheg in North; Tosk in the South (some Greek).

COMBAT EFFECTIVENESS
    Limited

ALGERIA

Defense Budget	$410,200,000
Population	14,600,000
Manpower in the Armed Forces	60,300
Defense as % of GNP	10%

ARMY

MANPOWER
    53,000 men (Reserves of 50,000)
GENERAL
    The armed forces consist of the National People's Army, including a small Navy, Air Force, and the National Gendarmerie.
    The Army is organized into five military regions - (Blida, Oran, Bechar, Quargla, and Constantine). Basic tactical unit is the battalion. There are: 50 infantry, 5 artillery, 1 anti-aircraft, 1 engineer, 1 paratroop, 3 tank battalions. Recently formed is 1 motorized division with 4 infantry brigades and 1 armored brigade.
PRINCIPAL EQUIPMENT
    Weapons: Light and Heavy Artillery
                    350 T-54, T-55, and AMX-13s
                    100 T-34 Tanks
                    400 Armored Personnel Carriers
    Missiles: Guideline SAM
                    Light and Heavy Artillery (est. 150 pcs.)

NAVY

MANPOWER
    3,300 men
GENERAL
    Primarily engaged in Coast Guard type duties.
PRINCIPAL EQUIPMENT
    Ships: 6 Coastal Escorts
                  10 Missile Boats
                  12 MTBs
                   2 Minesweepers
                   1 Trawler
    Missiles: Styx

AIR FORCE

MANPOWER
    4,000 men (reserve of 3,000)
GENERAL
    Operates out of 10 bases.

PRINCIPAL EQUIPMENT
    Aircraft: Interceptors   48 MiG-21s
                   Fighter-Bombers 20 MiG-15s
                                    70 MiG-17s
                                    20 Su-7s
                 Light-Bombers   24 Il-28s
                 Transports   8 An-12s
                                    12 Il-14s
                                    4 Il-18s
                 Helicopters   40 Mi-4s
                                    4 Mi-1s
                                    7 Hughes 269As
                                    5 SNIAS SA-330s
               Trainers   12 Yak-11s
                                  12 Gomhuriah Mk.2s
                                  2 Beech D18S
                                  3 MiG-15UTIs
                                  4 MiG-21UTIs
               Armed Trainers   28 Fouger Magisters
    Missiles: Guideline SAM
                 Atoll AAM

BASES
    Bishkro, Bou-Sfer, Oukda, Ouargla, Mere-el-Kebir, La Calle, Paul-Cazelles, Reggane, Zenate.

MISCELLANEOUS DATA

DEFENSE AGREEMENTS
    Arab League (Arab Defense Council, Unified Arab Command)
MAP TYPE ASSISTANCE RECEIVED FROM
    Cuba, Czechoslovakia, USSR, USR, France
INTERNAL SECURITY FORCES
    Gendarmerie - 10,000 men
CONSCRIPTION LAW
    All volunteer force
MILITARY SCHOOLS
    Officer training has been conducted in UAR and Soviet Union. Recently Soviet personnel handling MiG-21 flight and maintenance trained at Algerian bases. 1,500 Soviet personnel in country.
NATIONAL FLAG
    A red star and a red crescent superimposed on a background of green (left hand of flag) and white (right hand).
OFFICIAL LANGUAGE
    Arabic
COMBAT EFFECTIVENESS
    Excellent

ANGOLA

Defense Budget	N.A.
Population	6,166,000
Manpower in the Armed Forces	7,000
Defense as % of GNP	N.A.

ARMY

MANPOWER
    7,000 men (7,000 Civilian Militia)
PRINCIPAL EQUIPMENT
    Weapons: T-34/54 Tanks
                 PT-76 Armored Cars
                 122-mm Ground-to-Air Rockets
                 Mortars
                 Light and Medium Artillery
    Missiles: SAM-7
    Aircraft: MIG-21s
                 Spotter Aircraft
                 Helicopters

During the recent war for control of the Angolian government, the Soviet Union provided the MLPA forces with approximately $200-million in military aid.

The Soviet Union has 400 military advisors in Angola during the insurrection, and there was an estimated 12,000 Cuban military personnel in the country.

Cuban Air Force pilots manned the MIG-21s, spotter aircraft and helicopters.

Military assistance provided to the FNLA/UNITA forces by the United States was stated as being approximately $20-million.

No more current information on the organization or future of the new government's armed forces is available.

ARGENTINA

Defense Budget	$1,290,000,000
Population	23,539,000
Manpower in the Armed Forces	140,150
Defense as % of GNP	2.2%

ARMY

MANPOWER
   85,000 men (Reserves of 250,000)

GENERAL
   Organized into five military districts for administration. Four army corps consisting of five infantry, two mountain, one airborne, two mechanized brigades, plus 10 artillery regiments.
   Trained reserves are: 200,000 in National Guard and 50,000 Territorial Guards.
   The National Gendarmery, a constabulary force of 11,000 comes under control of the Commander-in-Chief of the Army.

PRINCIPAL EQUIPMENT
   Weapons: Light and Heavy Artillery
              120 M-4 Tanks
              120 AMX-13 Tanks
              250 M-113 Armored Personnel Carriers
   Aircraft: Transports   3 DHC-6 Otters
                              5 Beech Queens
                              1 King Air
              Liaison   11 Cessna U-17s
                              4 Piper Super Cubs
              Helicopters   7 Bell UH-1s
                              2 Bell 47Gs
                              7 Hiller FH-100s
   Missiles: Cobra ATM
              Tigercat

NAVY

MANPOWER
   34,150 men (includes Naval Aviation and Naval Infantry) (Marines)

GENERAL
   One of the largest fleets in South America. It is organized into six commands: Naval Shore Areas, Naval Aviation, Naval Infantry, Naval Transport, Hydrographic Service, and Naval Training Facilities.
   The National Maritime Prefecture - a Coast Guard type force of 8,000 is under the control of the Commander-in-Chief of the Navy.

PRINCIPAL EQUIPMENT
   Ships: 1 Aircraft Carrier
               4 Submarines
               3 Cruisers
              10 Destroyers (6 new ones to be ordered)
               2 Corvettes
               4 Coastal Minesweepers

ARGENTINA

	2 Minehunters	
	11 Patrol Vessels	
	3 Patrol Craft	
	3 Survey Ships	
	1 Training Ship	
	4 Transports	
	3 Oilers	
	5 LSTs	
	29 Landing Craft	
	1 Mine Support Vessel	
	1 Icebreaker	
	1 Salvage Vessel	
	13 Tugs	
Aircraft:	Attack	15 A4Q Skyhawks
		6 Aeromacchi MB 326s
	Reconnaissance	6 S-2A Trackers
		6 P-2H Neptunes
	Transports	3 Lockheed Electras
		7 C-47s
		6 C-54s
		2 DHC-6s
		5 Short Skyvans
		1 H.S. 125
	Helicopters	10 Bell 47s
		6 Alouette IIIs
		4 Sea King ASW
	Search/Rescue	3 HU-16B Albatross
Missiles:	Bantam ATGW	
	Tigercat SAM	
	Seacat	
	Seawolf	

AIR FORCE

MANPOWER
 21,000 men
GENERAL
 Organized into four key commands: Air Operations, Air Regions, Material and Personnel Commands.
 Air Operations Command is made up of 5 air brigades, each with up to 3 groups of squadron strength operating from a single base.
 Approximately 20 air bases in use.
PRINCIPAL EQUIPMENT

Aircraft:	Fighter-Bombers	12 Mirage IIIs
		45 A-4 Skyhawks
		19 F-86 Sabres
	Bombers	9 BAC Canberras
	Ground Attack	40 MS-760 Paris
		60 T-34 Armed Trainers
	Transports	6 C-45s
		3 DHC-2 Beavers
		3 DHC-3 Otters
		6 C-130 Hercules

```
                        11 F-27s
                         4 DC-6s
                        20 DH Doves
                        26 IA 50 GIIs
         Helicopters     5 Bell UH-1Hs
                         4 Bell 47Gs
                         3 Hiller UH-23s
                        11 Hughes OH-6As
                         6 Sikorsky S-55S
```

Missiles: Matra

BASES

Parana, El Palomar, Aeroparaque, Moron, Tandil, Entre Rios, Mendoza, San Luis, Sante Fe, Cordoba, Mar de Plata, Tierra del Fuega, Missiones, Santa Cruz, Puerto Deseedo, Chubut, Chebut, Rio Negro, Quilmes, Chamical.

MISCELLANEOUS DATA

DEFENSE AGREEMENTS
    Rio Pact
MAP TYPE ASSISTANCE RECEIVED FROM
    U.S.
INTERNAL SECURITY FORCES
    National Gendarmerie - 11,000
    National Maritime Prefecture - 8,000
CONSCRIPTION LAW
    Men 20 to 45 liable to compulsory service - 1 year in Army or Air Force and 2 years in Navy. All go into inactive reserve until age 50. The 1st line reserve are made up of men 20 thru 29, the 2nd line 30 thru 39, and 3rd line 40 thru 50 age brackets. It is estimated that there are close to one million in 1st line category in event of mobilization.
MILITARY SCHOOLS
    There are three officer academies: The Military Academy, The Naval Academy and The School of Military Aviation. There is also a National War College (joint).
    Army-Supervisor War School and the Center for Higher Studies. Navy: Post-Graduate School and Naval War College. Air Force: Command and General Staff School.
    There are a number of non-commissioned officer schools in all services, plus technical schools for enlisted personnel.
NATIONAL FLAG
    Sky-blue, white and sky-blue (equal, horizontal); with a rising sun on the white band.
OFFICIAL LANGUAGE
    Spanish
COMBAT EFFICIENCY
    Excellent
SPECIAL NOTES
    Country presently under effective military control due to internal political instability.

AUSTRALIA

Defense Budget	$1,961,800,000
Population	12,959,084
Manpower in the Armed Forces	68,720
Defense as % of GNP	5.1%

ARMY

MANPOWER
   31,000 men (Reserves of 26,577)

GENERAL
   A centralized Ministry of Defense has been established to assume many of the functions of the old separate departments.
   The former Regional and Territorial Commands have been replaced by Field Force, Logistic and Training Commands.
   Army has 9 infantry battalions; 1 tank, 3 cavalry, 4 artillery, 6 signal, 3 engineer, 1 anti-aircraft, 1 aviation regiment; plus other special purpose forces.

PRINCIPAL EQUIPMENT
   Weapons: 150+ Centurion Tanks
              300 Saladin and Ferret Armored Cars
              700+ M-113 Armored Personnel Carriers
              Light and Heavy Artillery
   Aircraft: Transports   11 GAF N-22 Nomads
              Helicopters   50 Bell 47Gs
                             65 Bell 206s
                              5 Alouette IIIs
              Liaison   18 Pilatus Porters
                              9 Cessna 180s
   Missiles: Redeye SAM

NAVY

MANPOWER
   16,000 men (Reserves of 7,600)

GENERAL
   The Navy operates with the Fleet Air Arm as an integral part of its total force.

PRINCIPAL EQUIPMENT
   Ships: 1 Aircraft Carrier
              4 Submarines
              3 Guided-Missile Destroyers
              4 Destroyers (Daring and Battle Class)
              6 Destroyer Escorts, ASW
              2 Oceanographic Vessels
              4 Minesweepers
              2 Minehunters
              1 Destroyer Tender
             20 Patrol Craft
              1 Survey Ship
              1 Small Survey Ship
              1 Fleet Tanker
              1 Supply Ship

		6 Service Craft
		8 Landing Craft
		1 Fast Troop Transport
Aircraft:	ASW	14 S-2E Trackers
	Fighter-Bombers	16 A-4G Skyhawks
	Helicopters	9 Bell UH-1Ds
		2 Westland Scouts
		25 Wessex AS.3LBs
		10 Sea King HAS.50s
	Trainers	10 MB.326Hs
		2 H.S. 748s
		4 TA-4G Skyhawks
Missiles:	Seacat SAM	
	Ikara	
	Tartar	
	Sidewinder	

AIR FORCE

MANPOWER
   21,720   (Reserves of 7,157)

GENERAL
   Operational Command is responsible for operations; Support Command is responsible for recruitment, training, supply and maintenance. Operates about 16 bases.

PRINCIPAL EQUIPMENT

Aircraft:	Fighter-Bombers	64 Mirage IIIs
	Strike/Reconnaissance	30 F-111s
	Reconnaissance	8 BAC Canberra
	Maritime Reconnaissance	10 P3-B Orions
		9 Sp-2H Neptunes
	Transport	24 C-130 Hercules
		2 BAC-111
		3 Dassault Falcons
		22 DHC-4 Caribous
		2 H.S. 748s
		20 C-47s
	Helicopters	50 Bell UH-1s
		10 Bell 206s
		11 Vertol CH-47Cs
	Trainers	37 CT-4s
		70 Aeromacchi MB.326s
		4 BAC Canberras
Missiles:	Sidewinder AAM	
	Matra AAM	

BASES
   Amberley, Butterworth, Darwin, Ease Sale, Edinburgh, Fairbairn, Laverton, Learmouth, Pearce, Point Cook, Tindal, Richmond, Townsville, Wagga, Williamtown, Maralinga, Woomera.

AUSTRALIA

MISCELLANEOUS DATA

DEFENSE AGREEMENTS
  ANZUS, Malaya, SEATO

MAP TYPE ASSISTANCE RECEIVED FROM
  U.S., U.K.

INTERNAL SECURITY FORCES

CONSCRIPTION LAW
  All males age 20 are liable for service; only about 6,900 called annually. Majority volunteers. Service: 2 years in regular Army and then 3 years in reserve.

MILITARY SCHOOLS
  Royal Military College, Officer Cadet School, Officer Training Unit (OTC), Australian Staff College, Royal Australian Naval College, Royal Australian Air Force Academy.

NATIONAL FLAG
  Blue field, with the Union Jack in the upper left corner; a large 7 pointed white star directly beneath, and five smaller white stars in the right half.

OFFICIAL LANGUAGE
  English

COMBAT EFFECTIVENESS
  Excellent

SPECIAL NOTES
  RAAF has two Mirage squadrons in Malaysia and Singapore.
  Papau New Guinea will be independent this year and Australia will continue to provide defense assistance to new government.

AUSTRIA

Defense Budget $310,000,000
Population   7,474,000
Manpower in the Armed Forces   13,000 (Conscripts-
                                                     25,000)
Defense as % of GNP   N.A.

DEFENSE ESTABLISHMENT

Austria's defense establishment involves two services: the Army and Air Force. The nation is committed to a policy of neutrality.

ARMY

MANPOWER
   10,000 Regulars (23,000 Conscripts)*   Reserve of over 100,000
GENERAL
   Organized into 3 mechanized brigades, four infantry brigades, one commando battalion, and four communications battalions.
PRINCIPAL EQUIPMENT
   Weapons: Est.   325 M-47/60 Tanks
                     120 Tank Destroyers
                     500 Armored Personnel Carriers
              Est.   150+ Artillery Pieces (109mm or larger)
                     250 Anti-tank Guns (85mm)

AIR FORCE

MANPOWER
   3,000 Regulars (2,000 Conscripts)*   Reserve of 1K
GENERAL
   Treaty restrictions limit right to utilize guided missiles.
PRINCIPAL EQUIPMENT
   Aircraft: Fighter-Bombers   39 SAAB-105s
               Transports   3 D.H. Beavers
                                  2 Short Skyvans
               Helicopters   5 Bell 47Gs
                                 22 Bell 204s
                                 12 Bell 206s
                                 10 Alouette IIIs
                                  2 OH-13s
                                  2 S-65Os
               Liaison   19 O-1Es
BASES
   Langenlebarn, Graz-Thalerhof, Aigen, Wiener-Neustadt, Horsching, Zeltweg, Schwaz, Klagenfurt-Annibichl.

* NOTE:
   Conscripts serve 6 months with an additional 2 months of reserve training.

AUSTRIA

MISCELLANEOUS DATA

DEFENSE AGREEMENTS
    Policy of neutrality.
MAP TYPE ASSISTANCE RECEIVED FROM
    Sweden
INTERNAL SECURITY FORCES
    12,000 Gendarmerie
CONSCRIPTION LAW
    All males 18-50 for 6 months.
MILITARY SCHOOLS

NATIONAL FLAG
    Red, white and red horizontal stripes with the national coat of arms centered on the white stripe.
OFFICIAL LANGUAGE
    German
COMBAT EFFECTIVENESS
    Limited

BAHRAIN

Defense Budget	N.A.
Population	216,078
Manpower in the Armed Forces	1,200
Defense as % of GNP	N.A.

ARMY

MANPOWER
   1,100 men
GENERAL
   Organized into 1 infantry battalion and 1 armored car squadron.
PRINCIPAL EQUIPMENT
   16 Saladin and Ferret armored cars
   Anti-tank Guns
   Mortars

Bahrain has no Navy or Air Force; however, police force operates several patrol boats and two helicopters.

MISCELLANEOUS DATA

MAP TYPE ASSISTANCE RECEIVED FROM
   U.K.
INTERNAL SECURITY FORCES
   500 men
CONSCRIPTION LAW
   Volunteer forces
TREATIES
   Arab League
OFFICIAL LANGUAGE
   Arabic
COMBAT EFFECTIVENESS
   Limited
SPECIAL NOTES
   They have leased former British Naval facility to U.S. making only permanent facility on the Persian Gulf.

BANGLADESH

Defense Budget	$77,000,000
Population	79,399,411
Manpower in the Armed Forces	26,500
Defense as % of GNP	N.A.

ARMY

MANPOWER
  25,000 men
GENERAL
  Organized into infantry brigades with 17 infantry battalions, 1 tank regiment, 3 artillery regiments, and 4 support units.
PRINCIPAL EQUIPMENT
  Weapons: Conventional   15 M-24 Tanks
             Some heavy artillery

NAVY

MANPOWER
  500 men
PRINCIPAL EQUIPMENT
  Vessels: 3 Patrol Boats
             1 Coast Guard Vessel

AIR FORCE

MANPOWER
  1,000 men
GENERAL
  Small force of 25 aircraft with limited combat capability.
PRINCIPAL EQUIPMENT
  Aircraft: Fighter-Bombers   10 MIG-21s
                               10 F-86s
             Transports   1 DHC-4
                               1 DC-6
                               1 An-24
                               3 An-26s
                               2 F-27s
             Helicopters   5 Alouette II
                               4 Mi-8s
                               2 Westland Essex

BASES
  Tezgaon, Kurmitola, Saidpur, Lalmonirhat, Ishurdi, Barisal, Chittagong, Cox Bazar, Jessore, Chiringa, Dohazari, Hathazari.

MISCELLANEOUS DATA

DEFENSE AGREEMENTS
  India
MAP TYPE ASSISTANCE RECEIVED FROM
  India, USSR

INTERNAL SECURITY FORCES
    16,000 man National Guard, 13,000 Bangladesh Rifles
CONSCRIPTION LAW
    Voluntary forces
OFFICIAL LANGUAGE
    Bengali
NATIONAL FLAG
    Rectangular in bottle green, with a red circle centered on the green body.
COMBAT EFFECTIVENESS
    Limited
SPECIAL NOTES
    Military coup in August of 1975 placed government under military control.

BELGIUM 21

Defense Budget	$1,276,000,000
Polulation	9,650,944
Manpower in the Armed Forces	89,400
Defense as % of GNP	3.3%

ARMY

MANPOWER
    65,000 men (Reserves of 10,000)
GENERAL
    Organized into 1 armored brigade, 3 mechanized brigades, 3 reconnaissance and 3 motorized infantry battalions, 3 artillery and 3 engineer battalions, 1 parachute regiment, 4 missile battalions.
PRINCIPAL EQUIPMENT
    Weapons: 140 M-47 Tanks
                    350 Leopard Tanks
                    125 Scorpion Tanks
                     12 M-41 Tanks
            1,100 Armored Personnel Carriers
                500+ Pieces of heavy artillery
    Aircraft: 75 Alouette IIIs
                    10 Dornier-27s
    Missiles: Lance
                   Hawk
                   Nord SS-11

NAVY

MANPOWER
    5,000 men (Reserves of 7,600)
PRINCIPAL EQUIPMENT
    Ships: 7 Ocean Minesweepers
                   9 Coastal Minesweepers
                 12 Inshore Minesweepers
                  2 Support Ships
                  2 Research Ships
                  4 ASW Escorts
    Helicopters: 2 HSS-1s
                      3 Alouette IIIs

AIR FORCE

MANPOWER
    19,400 men
GENERAL
    Comprises about 150 combat aircraft operating out of 9 bases.
PRINCIPAL EQUIPMENT
    Aircraft: Fighter-Bombers   44 F-104s
                                        36 Mirage VBAs
                  Interceptors   44 F-104s
                  Reconnaissance   20 Mirage VBRs

BELGIUM

Transports	12 C-130s
	2 DC-3s
	12 Pembroke
	2 Falcon 20s
	4 DC-6s
Helicopters	5 HSS-1s
	6 S-58s
Trainers	40 Potez-Magisters
	20 T-33s
	12 TF-104s
	34 Marchetti 260s
	7 Stampe SV-4s

<u>Missiles</u>:   Nike-Hercules
                 Sidewinder
                 Hawk

BASES
     Beauvechain, Bierset, Brasschaat, Brustem, Butsweilerhof, Coxyde, Florennes, Kleine Brogel, Melsborek, Gossoncourt, Gosselies, Werl.

<u>MISCELLANEOUS DATA</u>

DEFENSE AGREEMENTS
     NATO, Netherlands
INTERNAL SECURITY FORCES
     16,000 Gendarmerie
CONSCRIPTION LAW
     Compulsory service of 12-15 months for male citizens.
NATIONAL FLAG
     Vertical stripes of black, yellow and red.
OFFICIAL LANGUAGE
     French and Flemish
COMBAT EFFECTIVENESS
     Excellent
SPECIAL NOTES
     Belgium has extensive technical assistance program aimed at its former African territories.

BENIN
(Dahomey)

Defense Budget	$ 5,500,000
Population	3,191,628
Manpower in the Armed Forces	1,800
Defense as % of GNP	3%

ARMY

MANPOWER
   1,700 men

GENERAL
   Organized into 2 infantry battalions and small parachute-commando, reconnaissance, artillery units.

PRINCIPAL EQUIPMENT
   Weapons: Light Artillery
              Armored Cars

NAVY

None. (However, 2 motor vessels are operated as part of Army).

AIR FORCE

MANPOWER
   100 men

GENERAL
   Primarily transport only.

PRINCIPAL EQUIPMENT
   Aircraft: 1 C-47
               1 Aero Commander
               2 Broussard Liaison

MISCELLANEOUS DATA

DEFENSE AGREEMENTS
   France, Union Africaine et Malgache

MAP TYPE ASSISTANCE RECEIVED FROM
   France, Israel, U.S.

INTERNAL SECURITY FORCES
   1,700 men

CONSCRIPTION LAW
   All males liable for service for 18 months.

MILITARY SCHOOLS
   N.A.

NATIONAL FLAG
   Vertical green band on left, with the rest of the flag consisting of a broad yellow horizontal band over a red one of the same width.

OFFICIAL LANGUAGE
   French

COMBAT EFFECTIVENESS
   Extremely Limited

BENIN
(Dahomey)

SPECIAL NOTES
    Dahomey has undergone 5 coups and 11 heads of government since she gained independence from the French on August 1, 1960.
    On December 3, 1974, President Mathieu Kerekou declared the nation a "Marxist-Leninist state".

BHUTAN

Defense Budget	$ None
Population	953,487
Manpower in the Armed Forces	None
Defense as % of GNP	N.A.

Bhutan has no Armed Forces as such and operates with an Internal Security Force of 5,000. The country is under the protection of India and uses forces for border protection purposes.

MISCELLANEOUS DATA

DEFENSE AGREEMENTS
 India
INTERNAL SECURITY FORCES
 5,000 men
CONSCRIPTION LAW
 Compulsory service for all males 18 to 50.
NATIONAL FLAG
 Divided diagonally with red to the left and saffron to the right, with a green dragon outlined in white in the center.
OFFICIAL LANGUAGE
 Dzongha
COMBAT EFFECTIVENESS
 None

```
Defense Budget                    $ 35,000,000
Population                          5,716,718
Manpower in the Armed Forces           24,000
Defense as % of GNP                      3.7%
```

ARMY

MANPOWER
    18,000 men
GENERAL
    Regiments: 2 cavalry, 12 infantry, 2 motorized, 3 artillery, 2 ranger, 1 paratroop and 3 engineer battalions.
PRINCIPAL EQUIPMENT
    <u>Weapons</u>:   Conventional   M-113 and VM-706
                                          Armored Personnel
                                          Carriers
                    Light and Heavy Artillery

NAVY

None

AIR FORCE

MANPOWER
    6,000 men
GENERAL
    Small, but well equipped - 60+ combat aircraft.
PRINCIPAL EQUIPMENT

```
        Aircraft:    Fighter-Bombers    3 F-86s
                                       10 F-51Ds
                     Armed Trainers     6 T-28 COIN
                                       12 T-6s
                                       13 T-33s
                                       18 MB-326s
                     Trainers          18 T-23s
                                        6 T-41s
                                        8 T-21s
                     Transports         1 Beech King Air
                                       12 C-47s
                                        6 Convairs 440s
                                        3 Misc. Cessnas
                     Helicopters        3 Hiller OH-23s
                                       12 Hughes 500Ms
                     Liaison           14 Cessna 185s
                                        2 Cessna Centurions
```
BASES
    Charana, Coloapima, El Tejar, El Trompillo, La Florida, La Paz, Puerto Suarez, Santa Cruz.

BOLIVIA

MISCELLANEOUS DATA

DEFENSE AGREEMENTS
    Rio Pact
MAP TYPE ASSISTANCE RECEIVED FROM
    U.S.
INTERNAL SECURITY FORCES
    5,000 men
CONSCRIPTION LAW
    Universal military service for 12 months; however few called.
NATIONAL FLAG
    Red, yellow and green horizontal stripes, with national coat of arms on the yellow stripe.
OFFICIAL LANGUAGE
    Spanish
COMBAT EFFECTIVENESS
    Limited
SPECIAL NOTES
    In 1971, the military took control of the country under the (then) Col. Hugo Banzer Suarez.

Defense Budget	None
Population	608,656
Manpower in the Armed Forces	None
Defense as % of GNP	0

Botswana is the former British protectorate of Bechuanaland and has no armed forces per se.

MISCELLANEOUS DATA

DEFENSE AGREEMENTS
    OAU
INTERNAL SECURITY FORCES
    1,000 men
NATIONAL FLAG
    Blue field divided by a black horizontal band with a narrow white stripe above and below the band.
OFFICIAL LANGUAGE
    English (Tswana also used).
COMBAT EFFECTIVENESS
    None

BRAZIL

Defense Budget $ 1,548,000,000
Population   93,139,037
Manpower in the Armed Forces   192,000
Defense as % of GNP   6.5%

ARMY

MANPOWER
    120,000 men

GENERAL
    Organized into 1 armored and 7 infantry divisions.

PRINCIPAL EQUIPMENT
- Weapons: Conventional
  - 200 M-41 Tanks
  - 140 M-4 Tanks
  - 35 M-47 Tanks
  - 225 Armored Cars
  - 210 Armored Personnel Carriers
- Missiles:
  - Hawk
  - Roland
  - Wide Range of Artillery
- Aircraft:
  - 13 Bell helicopters
  - 15 Whirlwinds
  - 5 Wasps
  - 20 Cessna O-1A Liaison
  - 19 NIEVA L-9 Liaison
- Missiles:
  - 114mm Rocket
  - AT-108 Rocket

NAVY

MANPOWER
    40,000 men (plus 1,000 Marines)

PRINCIPAL EQUIPMENT
- Ships:
  - 1 Aircraft Carrier
  - 2 Cruisers
  - 21 Destroyers
  - 3 Destroyer Escorts
  - 5 Frigates
  - 9 Submarines
  - 10 Corvettes
  - 2 Coastal Minesweepers
  - 3 Seaward Defense Boats
  - 2 River Monitors
  - 6 River Gunboats
  - 4 Transports
- Missiles:
  - Seacat
  - Exocet
  - Ikara

Aircraft: Helicopters 6 SH-3Ds
8 SH-58s
6 Wasps
8 Hiller UH-4s
10 Whirlwinds
20 Hughes 200s
18 Bell 206Bs

AIR FORCE

MANPOWER
    32,000 men
PRINCIPAL EQUIPMENT
    Aircraft: Bombers   12 B-26Ks
              Fighter-Bombers   12 Mirage IIIs
                                   36 F-5s
                                   20 T-33s
              Counterinsurgency   30 T-6s
                                   25 T-37s
                                  112 Embraer 326s
              Reconnaissance   10 P-2Es
                                   12 Grumman S-2As
              Transports   2 BAC-111s
                                    1 Viscount
                                    7 Beech E-18s
                                   10 C-45s
                                   50 C-47s
                                    4 DC-6s
                                   25 DHC-5s
                                   80 Embraer 110s
                                    9 VC-95s
                                    7 C-130s
              Helicopters   6 Bell Iroquois
                                   11 Bell 206s
                                   40 Bell H-13s
                                   15 Bell 47Gs
                                    5 Sikorsky H-19s
    Missiles: Ikara
              Seacat
              Exocet
              Matra
BASES
    Santa Cruz, Fortaleza, Porto Alegre, Natal, Sao Pedro da Aldeia, Salvador, Belem, Recife, Cumbica, Campos dos Afonsos, Santos, Manauas, Brasilia, Santos Dumont, Pirassununga, Sao Jose dos Campos.

MISCELLANEOUS DATA

DEFENSE AGREEMENTS
    Rio Pact
MAP TYPE ASSISTANCE RECEIVED FROM
    U.S.

BRAZIL 31

INTERNAL SECURITY FORCES
    30,000 Carabineros
CONSCRIPTION LAW
    All males age 21 and over must serve one year.
NATIONAL FLAG
    Green, with a yellow diamond enclosing a blue globe containing 23 white stars and a white band inscribed with the words "Ordem e Progresso".
OFFICIAL LANGUAGE
    Portugese
COMBAT EFFECTIVENESS
    Excellent
SPECIAL NOTES
    Country effectively under military control since 1969.
    Brazil now has second capability to U.S. in aircraft production in this hemisphere.
    Under a $5-billion agreement West Germany will provide Brazil with a complete fuel-cycle nuclear capability (which ultimately gives them weapons capabilities).

BULGARIA

Defense Budget	$ 395,000,000
Population	8,821,746
Manpower in the Armed Forces	149,000
Defense as % of GNP	2.9%

ARMY

MANPOWER
   120,000 men (Reserves of 250,000)

GENERAL
   Organized into 8 motorized rifle divisions and 5 tank brigades.

PRINCIPAL EQUIPMENT
   Weapons: Conventional
              2,300 Tanks T-34, T-54, T-55, T-62
              2,000+ Armored Personnel Carriers
              1,000+ Artillery Pieces
   Missiles: Sagger
              Snapper
              Scud

NAVY

MANPOWER
   7,000 men (Reserves of 15,000)

PRINCIPAL EQUIPMENT
   Vessels: 2 Submarines
               2 Destroyers
              16 Patrol Vessels
              16 Motor Torpedo Boats
              20 Minesweepers
              15 Landing Craft
   Aircraft: 6 Mi-4 Helicopters
              12 MIG-17s For Recon

AIR FORCE

MANPOWER
   22,000 men (Reserves of 20,000)

GENERAL
   Operates about 250 combat aircraft.

PRINCIPAL EQUIPMENT
   Aircraft: Fighter-Bombers   140 MIG-17s and MIG-12s
               Interceptors   60 MIG-19s
                                  36 MIG-17s
               Reconnaissance   12 IL-28s
                                  24 MIG-17s and MIG-21s
               Helicopters   40 Mi-4s
                                   6 Mi-6s
               Transports   6 An-2s
                                  10 IL-14s
                                   3 Li-2s
                                   4 IL-18s
   Missiles: Guideline, Atoll

BULGARIA 33

BASES
   Bozhurishte, Vrajdebna, Karlovo, Varna, Plovdiz,
Stara Zagora, Burgas, Balchik, Tolbuhin, Silistra,
Ruse, Targoviste, Ternovo, Haskovo, Pleven, Kardzali.

MISCELLANEOUS DATA

DEFENSE AGREEMENTS
   Warsaw Pact
MAP TYPE ASSISTANCE RECEIVED FROM
   U.S.S.R.
INTERNAL SECURITY FORCES
   20,000 men plus People's Militia of 150,000
CONSCRIPTION LAW
   Men age 18 liable for 2 years' service in Army or
3 years in other services.
NATIONAL FLAG
   Horizontal stripes of white, green and red, with
the state emblem, a lion framed by wheatstalks, located
on the white stripe near the hoist.
OFFICIAL LANGUAGE
   Bulgarian
COMBAT EFFECTIVENESS
   Excellent
SPECIAL NOTES
   Bulgaria contributed troops to the invasion and
occupation of Czechoslovakia in 1968.

Defense Budget	$ 151,000,000
Population	28,885,867
Manpower in the Armed Forces	158,300
Defense as % of GNP	4.8%

ARMY

MANPOWER
  145,000 men

GENERAL
  Organized into 5 major commands; 110 infantry, 2 armored, 4 artillery and 1 engineer battalion.

PRINCIPAL EQUIPMENT
  Weapons: Conventional
            Comet Tanks
            Ferret and Humber Armored Cars
            Light and Heavy Artillery

NAVY

MANPOWER
  6,300 men

PRINCIPAL EQUIPMENT
  Vessels: 28 Motor Gunboats
             1 Frigate
             3 Patrol Boats
             5 Motor Torpedo Boats
             2 Patrol Vessels
             4 Support Gunboats
             9 Transports

AIR FORCE

MANPOWER
  7,000 men

GENERAL
  Primarily for internal security.

PRINCIPAL EQUIPMENT
  Aircraft: Fighter-Bombers   3 MIG-17s
             Counterinsurgency 10 AT-33s
                                1 DH Vampire
             Transports   2 Bristols
                                6 C-45s
                               20 C-47s
                                2 DH Otters
             Helicopters   10 Bell H-21s
                               13 Bell 47s
                                3 Vertol HH-43s
                               13 Alouette IIIs

BASES
  Mingaladon, Hinawbi, Meiktila, with many remote landing strips.

MISCELLANEOUS DATA

DEFENSE AGREEMENTS
 None - Policy of non-alignment
MAP TYPE ASSISTANCE RECEIVED FROM
U.S., U.S.S.R.
INTERNAL SECURITY FORCES
 42,000 men
CONSCRIPTION LAW
 Men 18 to 46, women 18 to 36, and all physicians, engineers and technicians 18 to 56 liable for service of 6 months to 2 years.
NATIONAL FLAG
 A red field with a blue rectangle in the upper left corner containing a 5-pointed white star surrounded by smaller, similar stars.
OFFICIAL LANGUAGE
 Burmese
COMBAT EFFECTIVENESS
 Limited
SPECIAL NOTES
 Country has been experiencing difficult years with widespread disorder and strikes - fighting on border near China (Shan state) intensified last year.
 Although a new Burmese Constitution was adopted in 1974, the government remains based on army leadership. Sixteen out of 18 cabinet officers are military or ex-military men.

Defense Budget	$ 6,000,000
Population	3,653,159
Manpower in the Armed Forces	1,300
Defense as % of GNP	N.A.

DEFENSE ESTABLISHMENT

The President is also Minister of Defense and Chief of the Armed Forces Staff, issues policy and guidance to the Commander of the Armed Forces, which is divided into combat, intervention and territorial units.

ARMY

MANPOWER
 1,300 men
GENERAL
 Organized into small infantry units; small paracommand unit of 150 men.
PRINCIPAL EQUIPMENT
 Weapons: Conventional

Burundi has no Navy or Air Force. Congolese aircraft were used for paracommando unit training; however, they have no aircraft under their direct control.

MISCELLANEOUS DATA

DEFENSE AGREEMENTS
 Belgium, OAU
MAP TYPE ASSISTANCE RECEIVED FROM
 Belgium, U.S.S.R.
INTERNAL SECURITY FORCES
 3,000 men in National Gendarmerie
CONSCRIPTION LAW
 Volunteer force
NATIONAL FLAG
 A white diagonal saltier or cross, on green and red quarters, with a circular white panel in the center bearing three red stars outlined in green.
OFFICIAL LANGUAGE
 Rundi, a Bantu tongue.
COMBAT EFFECTIVENESS
 Extremely Limited
SPECIAL NOTES
 Belgium has provided about 40 military advisors. Instability of country runs high and border problems with Rwanda afford potential problems for this fledgling nation.

CAMBODIA
(Khmer Republic)

Defense Budget	$ 105,000,000
Population	8,223,406
Manpower in the Armed Forces	220,000
Defense as % of GNP	8%

ARMY

MANPOWER
    200,000 men

GENERAL
    Organized into 5 infantry divisions, 1 armored brigade, 10 infantry brigades, 1 paracommand brigade, 1 artillery brigade.

PRINCIPAL EQUIPMENT
    <u>Weapons</u>:   Conventional
                  25 M-24 and AMX-13 Tanks
                  90 Armored Cars
                  200 Armored Personnel Carriers
                  Light and Heavy Artillery

NAVY

MANPOWER
    10,000 men (including Naval Infantry)

PRINCIPAL EQUIPMENT
    <u>Vessels</u>:   20 Patrol Craft
                  2 Patrol Vessels
                 50 Support Gunboats
                 30 Landing Craft
                 6 Seaward Patrol Craft

AIR FORCE

MANPOWER
    10,000 men

PRINCIPAL EQUIPMENT
    <u>Aircraft</u>:   Fighter-Bombers 6 Douglas A-1Ds
                   Counterinsurgency 45 T-28s
                                    24 Cessna A-37Bs
                                    6 C-47s
                 Helicopters   32 Bell UH-1Ds
                                    9 Alouette IIIs
                                    2 Sikorsky H-34s
               Transports   20 C-47s
                                    1 C-54
                                    8 DH Otters
                                    6 C-123s

BASES
    Pochentong, Angkor, Battambang.

CAMBODIA
(Khmer Republic)

MISCELLANEOUS DATA

DEFENSE AGREEMENTS
    U.S.
MAP TYPE ASSISTANCE RECEIVED FROM
    Red China, France, Japan, U.S., Yugoslavia
INTERNAL SECURITY FORCES
    150,000 men
CONSCRIPTION LAW
    Volunteer forces
MILITARY SCHOOLS
    Khmer Military School, School of Application, Infantry Training Center, Jungle Warfare School, Engineering School, Naval Instruction Center, Royal Flying School, Royal Khmer Military Academy.
NATIONAL FLAG
    Blue, with a red field in the upper left-hand corner containing an outline of the Angkor Wat temple and three white stars.
OFFICIAL LANGUAGE
    Cambodian or Khmer
COMBAT EFFECTIVENESS
    Limited
SPECIAL NOTES
    Although Prince Sihanouk has the titular role as Chief of State, control of government is principally in hands of Communist Khmers Rouges.

CAMEROON

Defense Budget	$ 29,000,000
Population	6,508,243
Manpower in the Armed Forces	5,500
Defense as % of GNP	6.0%

ARMY

MANPOWER
  5,000 men
GENERAL
  Organized into 4 infantry battalions, armored car squadron and paracommando unit.
PRINCIPAL EQUIPMENT
  Weapons: Conventional
            Armored Cars
            Light and Heavy Artillery

NAVY

MANPOWER
  200 men
PRINCIPAL EQUIPMENT
  Vessels: 4 Patrol Boats
            1 River Gunboat

AIR FORCE

MANPOWER
  300 men
PRINCIPAL EQUIPMENT
  Aircraft: 7 Broussards   1 Dornier 28
             5 C-47s   3 Dassault MD-315R
             2 Allouette IIIs 2 Beech Queen Air
                                 Liaison
BASES
  Yaounde, Douala, Batouri, Calabar, Garouna

MISCELLANEOUS DATA

DEFENSE AGREEMENTS
  France, Union Africaine et Malgache
MAP TYPE ASSISTANCE RECEIVED FROM
  France, U.S.
INTERNAL SECURITY FORCES
  9,000 men
CONSCRIPTION LAW
  Volunteer Forces
NATIONAL FLAG
  Vertical green, red and yellow stripes, with 2 yellow stars in the upper part of the green stripe.
OFFICIAL LANGUAGE
  Cameroonian
COMBAT EFFECTIVENESS
  Extremely Limited

CANADA

```
Defense Budget                  $ 3,050,000,000
Population                         22,998,000
Manpower in the Armed Forces           77,900
Defense as % of GNP                       2.4%
```

ARMY

MANPOWER
   28,500 men (Reserves of 20,000)
GENERAL
   Composed of 3 infantry battalions; 1 reconnaissance, 1 artillery, 1 airborne, 1 communications regiment.
PRINCIPAL EQUIPMENT
   Weapons: 200+ Centurion Tanks
               175 M-24 Tanks
               120 Ferret Armored Cars
               175 Lynx Reconnaissance Vehicles
               800+ M-113 APCs
               180 Leopard Tanks
               Light and Heavy Artillery
   Missiles: Entac
               Blowpipe
               Tow
               SS-11
   Aircraft: Helicopters   45 Bell CUH-1Ns
                                 70 Bell OH-58s
                                  9 Vertol CH-113s

NAVY

MANPOWER
   13,400 men (Reserves of 30,000)
PRINCIPAL EQUIPMENT
   Vessels: 19 Destroyer Escorts
                3 Submarines
                1 ASW Hydrofoil
                4 ASW Helicopter/Destroyers
                6 Coastal Minesweepers
                2 Escort Maintenance Ships
                6 Survey Ships
                3 Patrol Craft
                3 Supply Vessels
                2 Oilers
                6 Training Vessels
   Aircraft: 32 Sea King
               26 CP-107s
               18 P-3 Orions
                6 T-33s
               12 DH Trackers ASW
   Missiles: Sea Sparrow

CANADA

AIR FORCE

MANPOWER
  36,000 men (Reserves of 800)
PRINCIPAL EQUIPMENT
  Aircraft: Air Defense   58 CF-101s
                               60 F-104s
                               30 CF-100s
             Air Transport   24 C-130s
                                5 Boeing 707s
                                7 Falcons
                               14 Buffalos
                                8 Otters
                               10 Cosmopolitans
                                6 Labrador Helicopters
             Maritime Patrol   (see Navy)
             Mobile Command   18 F-5s
                                8 CH-47 Helicopters
                               72 Bell Kiowas

MISCELLANEOUS DATA

DEFENSE AGREEMENTS
  NATO
CONSCRIPTION LAW
  Volunteer Forces
INTERNAL SECURITY FORCES
  13,000 men
NATIONAL FLAG
  A narrow, vertical red stripe on either side of a broad white field containing a red maple leaf.
OFFICIAL LANGUAGE
  English
COMBAT EFFECTIVENESS
  Excellent
SPECIAL NOTES
  Canada has unified its armed services and although presented in separate sections, they are now one...The Canadian Armed Forces.
  Canada has been a major contributor of its military forces to UN peace-keeping missions.
  Canada and the United States cooperate closely on North American defense, chiefly via NORAD.

CENTRAL AFRICAN REPUBLIC

Defense Budget	$ 5,000,000
Population	1,630,983
Manpower in the Armed Forces	1,200
Defense as % of GNP	3.0%

ARMY

MANPOWER
   1,000 men
GENERAL
   Organized as infantry battalion.
PRINCIPAL EQUIPMENT
   Light Weapons - Armored Cars

NAVY

None.

AIR FORCE

MANPOWER
   200 men
GENERAL
   Small transport force with role of moving troops rapidly in time of need.
PRINCIPAL EQUIPMENT
   Aircraft:
   - Transports: 1 Dassault Falcon (Presidents' Aircraft)
                 3 C-47s
                 1 DC-4
   - Liaison: 10 Aeromacchi AL-60s
                 7 MH Broussards
   - Helicopters: 1 Alouette II
                  1 Bell 47G
                  10 Sikorsky H-34s
   - Fighters: 4 A-1D Skyraiders

MISCELLANEOUS DATA

DEFENSE AGREEMENTS
   Chad, France
MAP TYPE ASSISTANCE RECEIVED FROM
   France, Israel, U.S.
INTERNAL SECURITY FORCES
   1,500 men
CONSCRIPTION LAW
   Selective Service
MILITARY SCHOOLS
   None.
NATIONAL FLAG
   Four horizontal bands of blue, white, green and yellow, bisected by a vertical red bar, and a yellow five-pointed star at upper left.
OFFICIAL LANGUAGE
   French
SPECIAL NOTES
   In 1966, military took control of government and rules via a Revolutionary Council. General Jean-Bedel Bokassa assumed presidency after ouster of President Dacko.

CHAD

Defense Budget	$ 18,000,000
Population	3,500,000
Manpower in the Armed Forces	4,000
Defense as % of GNP	2.0%

DEFENSE ESTABLISHMENT

The President controls the armed forces through two cabinet-level assistants. The Minister of Defense directs the Army and its small air element and the National Gendarmerie, one of the two civil police forces. The Minister of the Interior directs the National Guard (Primarily a quasi-military guard force) and the Surete' Nationale.

ARMY

MANPOWER
    3,800 men

GENERAL
    Organized into three infantry and one mounted camel company. One parachute group.

PRINCIPAL EQUIPMENT
    Light Weapons
    Armored Cars
    Light Artillery

NAVY

None.

AIR FORCE

MANPOWER
    200 men

PRINCIPAL EQUIPMENT
    Aircraft:
        Transports   6 C-47s
                           10 Noratlas 2501s
        Liaison   3 MH Broussards
        Helicopters   1 Alouette II
                           10 Sikorsky H-34s

NATIONAL GENDARMERIE

MANPOWER
    1,600 men

NATIONAL GUARD

MANPOWER
    4,000 men

MISCELLANEOUS DATA

DEFENSE AGREEMENTS
    France, Central African Republic, Gabon, People's Republic of the Congo.
MAP TYPE ASSISTANCE RECEIVED FROM
    France, Israel, U.S., West Germany
INTERNAL SECURITY FORCES

CONSCRIPTION LAW
    Volunteer Forces
MILITARY SCHOOLS
    Officer's School at Ft. Lamy
NATIONAL FLAG
    Tricolor of blue, gold and red
OFFICIAL LANGUAGE
    French
COMBAT EFFECTIVENESS
    Limited
SPECIAL NOTES
    France maintains a force of about 800 troops at Fort Lamy with small air force contingent of about 50 aircraft.

CHILE

```
Defense Budget                $ 223,000,000
Population                     10,530,000
Manpower in the Armed Forces       60,000
Defense as % of GNP                  2.0%
```

ARMY

MANPOWER
    32,000 men
GENERAL
    Organized into 6 infantry brigades, 6 cavalry regiments, and 8 artillery regiments.
PRINCIPAL EQUIPMENT
    Weapons: 140 M-3 and M-41 Tanks
                Light and Heavy Artillery
                120 Armored Personnel Carriers

NAVY

MANPOWER
    14,000 men (including Marines)
PRINCIPAL EQUIPMENT
    Vessels: 3 Cruisers
                6 Destroyers
                4 Escorts
                2 Submarines
                1 Training Ship
                2 Transports
                6 Patrol Vessels
                6 Landing Craft
    Aircraft: 5 Bell 47G Helicopters
                3 C-47s
                5 C-45s
    Missiles: Seacat

AIR FORCE

MANPOWER
    14,000 men
PRINCIPAL EQUIPMENT
    Aircraft: Bombers   8 B-26s
                Fighter-Bombers 40 Hunter 71s
                                 15 F-5s
                ASW Patrol   5 Grumman HU-16s
                                  3 PBY-5s
                                  2 UH-D1s
                Transports   12 C-45s
                                  6 DC-6s
                                  2 C-130s
                                  8 DHC-6s
                                  8 C-47s
                                  4 C-118s

Helicopters	10 Puma SA-330s
	7 Bell OH-13s
	2 Sikorsky UH-19s
	16 Hiller OH-23s
	6 MBB 105s

BASES
    Iquique, Antofagasta, Quintero, El Bosque, Los Cerrillos, Temucho, Puerto Monti, Punta Arenas.

MISCELLANEOUS DATA

DEFENSE AGREEMENTS
    Rio Pact
MAP TYPE ASSISTANCE RECEIVED FROM
    U.K., U.S., U.S.S.R.
INTERNAL SECURITY FORCES
    30,000 men
CONSCRIPTION LAW
    All males between 20 and 45 are liable for service. Active reserve for 12 years and in secondary reserve until 45.
NATIONAL FLAG
    A white horizontal stripe over a longer red stripe, with a blue square in the upper left corner containing a 5-pointed white star.
OFFICIAL LANGUAGE
    Spanish
COMBAT EFFECTIVENESS
    Excellent
SPECIAL NOTES
    In September, 1973, the government was taken over by a military junta which currently has full control in all areas of government.
    Chile is reported to be negotiating for acquisition of Soviet MIG-21s.

CHINA
(COMMUNIST)

Defense Budget	$ 12,000,000,000*
Population	800,000,000
Manpower in the Armed Forces	3,250,000
Defense as % of GNP	10%

ARMY

MANPOWER
   2,845,000 (People's Militia of 5-7 Million)

GENERAL
   Composed of approximately 150 divisions, including 22 artillery, 6 armored, 3 cavalry, 2 airborne and the balance infantry.

PRINCIPAL EQUIPMENT
   Weapons: Light and Heavy Artillery
              Est. 2,000 Tanks   T-34, T-54, T-60, TK-61
              Armored Personnel Carriers
              Armored Cars
   Missiles: IRBM - 30
              MRBM - 55

NAVY

MANPOWER
   155,000 men (including 28,000 Marines and 16,000 Naval airmen)

GENERAL
   Comprises three fleets: North Sea, East Sea and South Sea.

PRINCIPAL EQUIPMENT
   Ships: 42 Submarines (some with rocket launchers)
               9 Destroyer Escorts
               6 Destroyers
              24 Submarine Chasers
             390 Motor Patrol Boats
              25 Motorized Missile Boats
              27 Minesweepers
              70 Landing Craft
             380 Miscellaneous Small Craft
   Aircraft: 100 Il-28s Torpedo Bombers
             400+ MiG-17s and 19s
              16 Tu-2s
                 Beriev Be-6s
              40 Mi-4s (ASW) Helicopters
   Missiles: SA-2 SAM

AIR FORCE

MANPOWER
   250,000 men

* See Special Notes

CHINA
(COMMUNIST)

GENERAL
Air Force operates ground air defense system; nuclear forces from 11 Military Regions. Currently operating over 4,500 aircraft.

PRINCIPAL EQUIPMENT

Aircraft:	Fighter-Bombers	750 MiG-15s	(F-2)**
		1,700 MiG-17s	(F-4)**
		1,000 MiG-19s	(F-9)**
		300 MiG-21s	(F-8)**
Bombers:	Bombers	100 Tu-16**	
		250 Il-28s	
	Transports	An-2**	
		Il-14	
		Il-18	
	Helicopters	Mi-1	
		Mi-4	
Missiles:	Atoll		
	Guideline		
	French R530		

MISCELLANEOUS DATA

DEFENSE AGREEMENTS

MAP TYPE ASSISTANCE RECEIVED FROM

INTERNAL SECURITY FORCES
250,000 men

CONSCRIPTION LAW
Provides for either 3 years service in Army or Security Forces, 4 years in Air Force or 5 years in Navy.

MILITARY SCHOOLS
Academy of Military Sciences

NATIONAL FLAG
Red, with 5 stars.

OFFICIAL LANGUAGE
Chinese

COMBAT EFFECTIVENESS
Excellent

SPECIAL NOTES
* Chinese defense budgets have not been public since 1960. Similarly to the Soviets, Red China has some defense expenditures included under non-defense items in the budget. For example, a Ministry for Heavy Industry shows in the general budget, but has under it a Bureau of Arsenals. Several Ministries of Machine Building show up as concerned with defense production. Similarly, various reports indicate that expenditures for military education and training were included in "cultural and educational" expenditures, while welfare and pension funds for military personnel were regarded as a part of "social service"

CHINA
(COMMUNIST)

expenditures. This projection is based upon current defense spending as being 10% of GNP.
** Each of these aircraft are manufactured in Chinese aircraft plants. Estimates are that they can produce: 270 MiG-19s; 30 Tu-16s; 80 MiG-21s annually with present plants.

Soviet troops totalling 45 divisions are now stationed in Asia Soviet republics and in the Mongolian People's Republic. Soviet forces have close to 20 Missile launchers for atomic weapons near the Soviet-Chinese border.

In 1973, China imported five times more aircraft over any prior years ... 12,400. Of this number, over 5,575 came from Japan.

Japanese TK-61 tanks, tank guns, anti-tank guns, complete artillery assembly plants, including helicopters, Mirage fighters and missiles are being procured from French.

Discussions with French, West German, Romanian, Yugoslavian, British aircraft and engine firms leading to possible licenses for modern aircraft and engines are underway.

Red China is estimated to have on-line today over 45 MRBM/IRBMs and nuclear weapons capabilities in light and medium bombers. ICBM capability will become operational in 1976.

Defense Budget	$ 120,000,000
Population	25,511,000
Manpower in the Armed Forces	63,000
Defense as % of GNP	2.5%

ARMY

MANPOWER
    50,000 men

GENERAL
    Organized into 10 infantry brigades; 1 airborne battalion, 20 motorized infantry, 5 artillery and support units.

PRINCIPAL EQUIPMENT
    Weapons: Conventional
                30 M-3 and M-4 Tanks
                50 M-8 and M-20 Armored Cars
                120 Armored Personnel Carriers
                Light and Heavy Artillery

NAVY

MANPOWER
    7,000 men (plus 800 Marines)

PRINCIPAL EQUIPMENT
    Vessels: 4 Destroyers
                4 Submarines (mini)
                4 Destroyer Escorts
                2 Oilers
                4 River Gunboats
                2 Tenders
                8 Coast Guard Vessels
                20 Patrol Launches

AIR FORCE

MANPOWER
    6,000 men

PRINCIPAL EQUIPMENT
    Aircraft: Fighter-Bombers   14 Mirage Vs
                                    4 Mirage IIIs
                                    5 F-5s
                Reconnaissance   3 B-26s
                                    2 RT-33s
                Helicopters   16 Bell 47s
                                   12 OH-6As
                                    6 TH-55s
                                    6 HH-43s
                                    6 UH-1Bs
                Transports   13 DHC-2s
                                    1 F-28
                                    2 HS-784s
                                    4 C-47s
                                   10 C-54s
                                    2 C-130s
                                    4 DHC-3s

COLOMBIA

BASES
   Cali, German Olano, Melgar, Luis F. Gomez Nino, Techo, Monteria, Berastegul, Pasto.

MISCELLANEOUS DATA

DEFENSE AGREEMENTS
   Rio Pact

MAP TYPE ASSISTANCE RECEIVED FROM
   U.S.

INTERNAL SECURITY FORCES
   35,000 men

CONSCRIPTION LAW
   One years' service between 18 and 30; reserve duty until 45.

NATIONAL FLAG
   The top half of the flag is yellow; the bottom half consists of a blue stripe and a red stripe of equal widths.

OFFICIAL LANGUAGE
   Spanish

COMBAT EFFECTIVENESS
   Excellent

SPECIAL NOTES
   Because of increased insurgent activity, country was placed under a "state of siege" order as of June 26, 1975.

CONGO
(Republic of the Congo)

Defense Budget	$ 20,000,000
Population	1,250,000
Manpower in the Armed Forces	5,350
Defense as % of GNP	5.0%

DEFENSE ESTABLISHMENT

The President, as commander-in-chief of the armed forces, is responsible for overall national defense and state security, has direct authority over the chief of staff of the Army, an officer in whom functional and operational control of the armed forces is vested. The headquarters of the Army, in Brazzaville, includes a general staff patterned after that in the French Army, as well as a political directorate, headed by a political commissar.

The Navy, the Air Force and the six operational defense zones into which the country was divided were subordinate to the Army Headquarters. The military zone in turn controlled various elements of the roughly five battalions that formed the tactical element of the Army.

ARMY

MANPOWER
   5,000 men
GENERAL
   Organized into one armored regiment, one infantry and one commando battalion; one engineer battalion, one recon squadron and an artillery group.
PRINCIPAL EQUIPMENT
   Light Weapons
   T-62, PT-76 Tanks
   Armored Personnel Carriers
   Light Artillery

NAVY

MANPOWER
   200 men
PRINCIPAL EQUIPMENT
   12 River Patrol Boats

AIR FORCE

MANPOWER
   150 men
PRINCIPAL EQUIPMENT
   Aircraft: Transports   2 C-47s
                               3 An-24s
               Liaison   3 MH Broussards
               Helicopters   3 Alouette IIs
                               1 Alouette III

CONGO
(Republic of the Congo)

MISCELLANEOUS DATA

DEFENSE AGREEMENTS
    France, Central African Republic, Chad, Gabon.
MAP TYPE ASSISTANCE RECEIVED FROM
    France, Cuba, Red China
INTERNAL SECURITY FORCES
    1,500 National Gendarmerie
    2,500 National Guard
CONSCRIPTION LAW
    Volunteer forces.
MILITARY SCHOOLS

NATIONAL FLAG
    Green and red triangles, separated by a diagonal yellow stripe.
OFFICIAL LANGUAGE
    French
COMBAT EFFECTIVENESS
    Limited
SPECIAL NOTES
    Army took control of government after coup in 1968.

Defense Budget	$ 8,000,000
Population	1,902,000
Manpower in the Armed Forces	1,200
Defense as % of GNP	.9%

ARMY

MANPOWER
    1,200 men
GENERAL
    Organized as Civil Guard only - the Army was abolished in 1948.

NAVY

MANPOWER
    35 men
GENERAL
    Operates as part of Coast Guard.
PRINCIPAL EQUIPMENT
    Vessels: 2 Motor Launches
                8 Small Craft

AIR FORCE

None.

MISCELLANEOUS DATA

DEFENSE AGREEMENTS
    Rio Pact
MAP TYPE ASSISTANCE RECEIVED FROM
    U.S.
INTERNAL SECURITY FORCES
    3,000 men
CONSCRIPTION LAW
    None.
NATIONAL FLAG
    A blue stripe at top and bottom, separated by two white stripes from a broad center red stripe bearing the national coat of arms on the left-hand side.
OFFICIAL LANGUAGE
    Spanish
COMBAT EFFECTIVENESS
    None

CUBA

Defense Budget	$ 300,000,000
Population	9,470,199
Manpower in the Armed Forces	121,000
Defense as % of GNP	6.3%

ARMY

MANPOWER
   90,000 men (plus 250,000 reserves)

GENERAL
   Organized into 1 artillery, 2 armored, and 9 infantry brigades.

PRINCIPAL EQUIPMENT
   Weapons: 700+ T-34, T-54, T-55, JS-2 Tanks
              250 Armored Personnel Carriers
              50   Armored Cars
                   Light and Heavy Artillery
   Missiles: Snapper AT

NAVY

MANPOWER
   6,000 men

PRINCIPAL EQUIPMENT
   Vessels: 3 Frigates
              2 Escorts
              24 PT Boats
              14 Motor Gunboats
              8 Motor Launches
              13 Coast Guard Vessels
              18 Missile Boats
   Aircraft: 18 Mi-4 Helicopters
   Missiles: Samlet

AIR FORCE

MANPOWER
   25,000 men

PRINCIPAL EQUIPMENT
   Aircraft: Fighter-Bombers   20 MIG-15s
                                70 MIG-17s
                                40 MIG-19s
                                80 MIG-21s
                                6 Su-7s
              Transports   60 Il-14s, An-2s, An-24s
              Helicopters   45 Mi-1s and Mi-4s
                                11 Bell 47s
                                3 Hiller 12As
                                3 Whirlwinds
   Missiles: Guideline
              Atoll

BASES
   Santa Clara, Camguey, San Antonio, San Julian, Hulguin, Santiago, Varadere, Havana, Camp Libertad.

MISCELLANEOUS DATA

MAP TYPE ASSISTANCE RECEIVED FROM
    U.S.S.R.

INTERNAL SECURITY FORCES
    15,000 men (also 200,000 men/women in People's Militia)

CONSCRIPTION LAW
    Compulsory service of 3 years for all men and women.

NATIONAL FLAG
    Three horizontal blue stripes separated by two white stripes, with an equilateral red triangle at the left containing a 5-pointed white star.

OFFICIAL LANGUAGE
    Spanish

COMBAT EFFECTIVENESS
    Excellent

SPECIAL NOTES
    Cuba is only American hemisphere government aligning itself closely with U.S.S.R. interests.
    Cuban military forces numbering over 6,000 were directly involved in Angola. Many are still in Africa assisting in training of guerrilla forces.

CYPRUS

Defense Budget	$ 10,000,000
Population	668,989
Manpower in the Armed Forces	2,000
Defense as % of GNP	2.0%

SPECIAL NOTES

In normal times, Cyprus has an authorized National Guard of 2,000 men, as well as 2,000 armed policemen. The figures above relate to these forces.

In July of 1974, Turkish forces invaded the island and seized the northern portion of the country including about 40% of the total land area of Cyprus.

Militarily, the Greek Cypriots are outnumbered three to one by the Turkish forces in terms of numbers of trained and equipped men, and as much as ten to one in important heavy equipment and artillery and armored vehicles.

Supervising the truce in Cyprus is a United Nations peace-keeping force of 3,548 men; from Australia - 35; Austria - 381; Canada - 522; Denmark - 432; Finland - 574; Ireland - 6; Sweden - 584; and Great Britain - 1,014.

Attempts have been made to negotiate under a formula which would set up a Turkish Zone encompassing 20% of the island - roughly proportionate to the Turkish percentage of total population. However, the Turks have refused to use percentage of population as an index to land jurisdiction.

The Turks have made it clear that because of past experiences, they will not permit repatriation of Greek Cypriot refugees in such numbers that the Turks would once again constitute a minority in any community in their zone.

Thus, an impasse exists and talks scheduled in New York for September 8, 1975 collapsed.

MISCELLANEOUS DATA

INTERNAL SECURITY FORCES
    2,000 men
CONSCRIPTION LAW
    Compulsory service for 6 months.
NATIONAL FLAG
    An outline map of Cyprus in gold above crossed green olive branches on a white field.
OFFICIAL LANGUAGE
    Greek and Turkish
COMBAT EFFECTIVENESS
    Negligible

CZECHOSLOVAKIA

Defense Budget $ 1,714,000,000
Population 14,875,000
Manpower in the Armed Forces 200,000
Defense as % of GNP 5.8%

ARMY

MANPOWER
    155,000 men (Reserves of 750,000)
GENERAL
    Organized into 5 tank, 1 motorized infantry divisions, 1 airborne brigade, plus support units.
PRINCIPAL EQUIPMENT
    Weapons: 100 JS-3/T-10 Tanks
                3500 T-55/62 Tanks
                  40 PT-76 Tanks
                2000 Armored Personnel Carriers
                1400 Artillery Pieces
                 200 Anti-tank Guns
    Missiles: Scud
                Snapper
                Swatter
                Sagger
                Guideline
                Frog

NAVY

None.

AIR FORCE

MANPOWER
    45,000 men (Reserves of 90,000)
PRINCIPAL EQUIPMENT
    Aircraft: Fighter-Bombers   160   Su-7s
                                  100+ MIG-17s
                Interceptors   80   MIG-19s
                                  150+ MIG-21s
                Reconnaissance   70   MIG-21s
                                   11   IL-28s
                Transports   60   An-24, Il-14, Il-28s
                Helicopters   100   Mi-1,4,8s
    Missiles: SA-2s
BASES
    Prague, Kosice, Zatec.

MISCELLANEOUS DATA

DEFENSE AGREEMENTS
    Warsaw Pact

CZECHOSLOVAKIA

MAP TYPE ASSISTANCE RECEIVED FROM
   U.S.S.R

INTERNAL SECURITY FORCES
   40,000 men in Border Guard, 120,000 in People's Militia.

CONSCRIPTION LAW
   2 years' compulsory service for all males 17 to 60 plus reserve time.

NATIONAL FLAG
   Blue triangle on the left with its apex toward the center; the rest of the flag consists of a white band on top and a red band on the bottom.

OFFICIAL LANGUAGE
   Czech and Slovak

COMBAT EFFECTIVENESS
   Excellent

SPECIAL NOTES
   Since the Soviet occupation in 1968, animosity toward the U.S.S.R. continues throughout the country.
   There are five Soviet Army Divisions stationed in the country.

Defense Budget $ 584,000,000
Population   5,133,250
Manpower in the Armed Forces   38,000
Defense as % of GNP   2.8%

ARMY

MANPOWER
    21,000 men (55,000 Reserves)
GENERAL
    Organized into 4 armored infantry brigades, 3 artillery battalions, and 1 battalion group.
PRINCIPAL EQUIPMENT
    Weapons: 200 Centurion Tanks
                 120 Leopard Tanks; M-41s
                 600+ M-113 Armored Personnel Carriers
                 Light and Heavy Artillery
    Missiles: Honest John
                 TOW AT

NAVY

MANPOWER
    7,000 men (4,000 Reserves)
PRINCIPAL EQUIPMENT
    Vessels: 2 Destroyers
                 6 Submarines
                 2 Patrol Vessels
                 7 Minelayers
                 8 Coastal Minesweepers
                 4 Inshore Minesweepers
                 16 Motor Torpedo Boats
                 9 Seaward Defense Boats
                 12 Patrol Craft
                 10 Landing Craft
                 1 Royal Yacht
    Aircraft: 8 Alouette III Helicopters

AIR FORCE

MANPOWER
    10,000 men (7,000 Reserves)
PRINCIPAL EQUIPMENT
    Aircraft: Fighter-Bombers   20 Draken
                                    46 F-100s
                Interceptors   40 F-104s
                                    40 Draken
                Reconnaissance   23 Draken
                Helicopters   8 Alouette IIIs
                                  8 Sikorsky S-61s
                Transports   3 C-130s
                                  8 C-47s
                                5 C-54s

DENMARK

    <u>Missiles</u>:   Sidewinder
                   Bullpup
                   Hawk
                   Nike Hercules

BASES
    Karup, Vaerlose, Skrydetrup, Aalborg, Avno, Vandel.

MISCELLANEOUS DATA

DEFENSE AGREEMENTS
    NATO
MAP TYPE ASSISTANCE RECEIVED FROM
    U.S.
INTERNAL SECURITY FORCES
    65,000 Home Guards
CONSCRIPTION LAW
    Compulsory service of 16 months for all males 19 to 25.
NATIONAL FLAG
    A white cross on red field.
OFFICIAL LANGUAGE
    Danish
COMBAT EFFECTIVENESS
    Excellent
SPECIAL NOTES
    Although active member of NATO, Denmark has imposed same limitations as Norway has on their participation - no foreign troops or nuclear weapons may be stationed on their territory.

Defense Budget	$ 37,000,000
Population	4,826,526
Manpower in the Armed Forces	16,300
Defense as % of GNP	4.0%

ARMY

MANPOWER
   9,000 men
GENERAL
   Organized into 3 infantry brigades, 1 artillery battalion, 1 anti-aircraft battalion.
PRINCIPAL EQUIPMENT
   Weapons: Conventional
                  20 Armored Cars
                  25 Armored Personnel Carriers

NAVY

MANPOWER
   3,800 men
PRINCIPAL EQUIPMENT
   Vessels: 3 Frigates
                 2 Corvettes
                 7 Patrol Vessels
                 2 Landing Craft
                 4 Coast Guard Vessels
                 3 Motor Launches

AIR FORCE

MANPOWER
   3,500 men
PRINCIPAL EQUIPMENT

Aircraft:		
	Bombers	3 B-26s
	Fighter-Bombers	10 DH Vampires
		20 F-51s
	Transports	5 C-47s
		6 C-46s
		3 DHC-2s
		3 Cessna 170s
	Helicopters	2 Bell 47s
		2 Hiller UH-12s
		3 Alouette IIs, IIIs
		7 Hughes OH-6s

BASES
   Santo Domingo

DOMINICAN REPUBLIC

MISCELLANEOUS DATA

DEFENSE AGREEMENTS
    Rio Pact
MAP TYPE ASSISTANCE RECEIVED FROM
    U.S.
INTERNAL SECURITY FORCES
    10,000 men
CONSCRIPTION LAW
    Compulsory service of 2 years for all males age 18.
NATIONAL FLAG
    Four rectangular sections divided by a white cross bearing the national coat of arms in the center; the upper left and lower right sections are dark blue and the other two red.
OFFICIAL LANGUAGE
    Spanish
COMBAT EFFECTIVENESS
    Limited

ECUADOR

Defense Budget $51,000,000
Population 6,916,853
Manpower in the Armed Forces 19,000
Defense as % of GNP 3.2%

ARMY

MANPOWER
    12,800 men
GENERAL
    Composed of 11 infantry battalions, 3 artillery groups, 3 mechanized squadrons, 2 snapper battalions, 2 AA battalions, 3 signal companies and independent units.
PRINCIPAL EQUIPMENT
    <u>Weapons</u>:   Light Artillery
                     51 Tanks - M-1, M-4, AMX-13s
                     Armored Cars
                     5 Liaison Aircraft

NAVY

MANPOWER
    3,700 men
PRINCIPAL EQUIPMENT
    <u>Vessels</u>:   1 Destroyer Escort
                       2 Escorts
                       2 Patrol Vessels
                       2 Patrol Boats
                       2 Landing Craft
                       3 PT Boats
                       1 Supply Ship
                       1 Survey Ship
                       1 Water Carrier

AIR FORCE

MANPOWER
    3,500 men
PRINCIPAL EQUIPMENT
    <u>Aircraft</u>:   Fighters   8 Gloster Meteors
                       COIN   8 BAC-167s
                       Bombers   5 Canberras
                       Transports   12 C-45/47s
                                       4 DC-6s
                                       2 Skyvans
                                       3 HS-748s

MISCELLANEOUS DATA

DEFENSE AGREEMENTS
    Rio Pact
MAP TYPE ASSISTANCE RECEIVED FROM
    U.S.

ECUADOR

INTERNAL SECURITY FORCES
    5,800 men
CONSCRIPTION LAW
    2 years' compulsory service.
NATIONAL FLAG
    Half of the width of the flag is yellow and the remaining half consists of blue and red bands; in the center is the national coat of arms.
OFFICIAL LANGUAGE
    Spanish
COMBAT EFFECTIVENESS
    Limited

EGYPT
(United Arab Republic)

Defense Budget	$ 3,500,000,000*
Population	33,329,000
Manpower in the Armed Forces	349,000
Defense as % of GNP	35%

ARMY

MANPOWER
    180,000 men (Reserves of 350,000)
    130,000 men in National Guard

GENERAL
    Organized into 3 armored and 4 mechanized infantry, plus 5 conventional infantry divisions; 2 airborne, 25 commando, 1 parachute, 4 artillery, 3 mortar brigades. Three SSM regiments.

PRINCIPAL EQUIPMENT

    <u>Weapons</u>: Light and Heavy Artillery (2,700 pieces)
                 Over 2,400 SAM Ba-teries
                 Over 3,000 Armored Personnel Carriers
                 Over 150 SA

    <u>Missiles</u>: Snapper   <u>Tanks</u>: 600 T-62s
                 Samlet   1900 T-54/55s
                 Strela   600 JS-3/T10s
               Guideline
               Goa
               Gainful

NAVY

MANPOWER
    14,000 men (Reserves of 15,000)

PRINCIPAL EQUIPMENT
    <u>Ships</u>:   12 Submarines
                 5 Destroyers
                 4 Escorts
                 1 Corvette
                 4 Fleet Minesweepers
                 2 Inshore Minesweepers
                36 Motor Torpedo Boats
                19 Missile Boats
                12 Sub Chasers
                14 Landing Craft
                 4 Tugs
                 2 Yachts
                 1 Transport
    <u>Missiles</u>: Styx

AIR FORCE

MANPOWER
    25,000 men (Reserves of 20,000)

* See Special Notes

EGYPT
(United Arab Republic)

GENERAL
Following massive losses in Israeli War, the UAR Air Force has been re-equipped and has close to 775 combat aircraft.

PRINCIPAL EQUIPMENT

Aircraft:	Fighter-Bombers	300	MiG-21s
		100	MiG-17s
		100	MiG-19s
	Fighters	150	MiG-21s
	Bombers	130	Su-7s
		26	Tu-16s
		9	Il-28s
	Transports	30	An-12s
		40	Il-14s
		3	An-24s
	Helicopters	85	Mi-1s & 4s
		20	Mi-6s
		70	Mi-8s
		8	Westland Mk-1s
		2	Westland Sea Kings
Missiles:	Atoll		
	Kelt		

MISCELLANEOUS DATA

DEFENSE AGREEMENTS
Arab League Collective Security Pact, Arab Unified Command

MAP TYPE ASSISTANCE RECEIVED FROM
Czechoslovakia, U.K., U.S., U.S.S.R., Saudi Arabia, Kuwait, Qatar, Abu Dhabi, Red China, Libya

INTERNAL SECURITY FORCES
90,000 men

CONSCRIPTION LAW
3 years compulsory service for all male citizens

MILITARY SCHOOLS
Military Academy, Naval Academy, Air Force Academy, Military Technical College, Army Staff Academy, Senior Officers Institute

NATIONAL FLAG
Red, white and black horizontal stripes with two 5-pointed green stars on the white stripe.

OFFICIAL LANGUAGE
Arabic

COMBAT EFFECTIVENESS
Excellent

SPECIAL NOTES
Egypt's own defense budget is only about 50% of the listed figure -- balance was funded by other Arab States out of oil bonanza, to replace equipment lost in war with Israel.

Soviet military advisors have left Egypt at President Sadat's request.

All plans calling for the union of Egypt and Libya have been cancelled.

Defense Budget $ 15,000,000
Population 4,277,000
Manpower in the Armed Forces 5,625
Defense as % of GNP 1.6%

ARMY

MANPOWER
   4,500 men (National Guard of 30,000)
GENERAL
   Organized into 1 artillery, 1 cavalry and 9 infantry regiments, for a total of 3 territorial divisions.
PRINCIPAL EQUIPMENT
   Weapons: Conventional
              18 Armored Cars
              Light Artillery

NAVY

MANPOWER
   125 men
PRINCIPAL EQUIPMENT
   Vessels: 2 Patrol Vessels
              3 Small Craft

AIR FORCE

MANPOWER
   1,000 men
PRINCIPAL EQUIPMENT
   Aircraft: Bombers   3 B-26s
              Fighter-Bombers   4 F-4s
                                6 F-51s
              Transports   4 C-47s
                                1 DC-4

MISCELLANEOUS DATA

DEFENSE AGREEMENTS
   Rio Pact
MAP TYPE ASSISTANCE RECEIVED FROM
   U.S.
INTERNAL SECURITY FORCES
   2,500 men
CONSCRIPTION LAW
   Compulsory service of 1 year for males 18 to 30.
NATIONAL FLAG
   Blue, white and blue horizontal stripes; with the national coat of arms centered on the white stripe.
OFFICIAL LANGUAGE
   Spanish
COMBAT EFFECTIVENESS
   Limited
SPECIAL NOTES
   Country has been facing increasing internal strife since 1974.

ETHIOPIA

Defense Budget	$ 85,000,000
Population	27,960,000
Manpower in the Armed Forces	44,000
Defense as % of GNP	3.1%

ARMY

MANPOWER
    40,000 men
GENERAL
    3 divisions with three 3-battalion brigades and supporting arms and services, 1 tank battalion, 1 medium artillery battalion, 3 AA batteries, 1 engineer battalion, 1 airborne infantry battalion and service units.
PRINCIPAL EQUIPMENT
    <u>Weapons</u>:   Conventional
                50 M-41 Light Tanks
                40 Armored Personnel Carriers
                85 Armored Cars
                Light Artillery

NAVY

MANPOWER
    1,400 men
PRINCIPAL EQUIPMENT
    <u>Vessels</u>:   3 Patrol Boats
                5 Motor Torpedo Boats
                1 Training Ship
                3 Landing Craft
                4 Harbor Defense Craft

AIR FORCE

MANPOWER
    3,000 men
PRINCIPAL EQUIPMENT
    <u>Aircraft</u>:   Fighter-Bombers   12 F-86s
                                    12 F-5s
                COIN   8 SAAB 17s
                Reconnaissance   8 RT-33s
                Helicopters   7 Alouette IIs
                                    5 Alouette IIIs
                Transports   6 C-47s
                                    2 C-54s
                                    3 DH Doves
BASES
    Debre Zeit, Bishoftu, Djidjigga, Asmara, Bahar Dar.

MISCELLANEOUS DATA

DEFENSE AGREEMENTS
    Kenya

MAP TYPE ASSISTANCE RECEIVED FROM
   India, Israel, Sweden, U.S.
INTERNAL SECURITY FORCES
   24,500 men
CONSCRIPTION LAW
   Volunteer forces
NATIONAL FLAG
   Green, yellow and red horizontal stripes; in the center, in orange, is a crowned lion bearing in its right forepaw a cross-staff with a national banner.
OFFICIAL LANGUAGE
   Amharic
COMBAT EFFECTIVENESS
   Limited
SPECIAL NOTES
   On September 12, 1974, a military coup took control of government and Emperor Haile Selassie was removed from power.
   In October, 1973, Ethiopia severed diplomatic relations with Israel.

FINLAND

Defense Budget	$ 250,000,000
Population	4,689,000
Manpower in the Armed Forces	35,300
Defense as % of GNP	2.6%

ARMY

MANPOWER
    30,000 men (Reserves of 600,000+)

GENERAL
    Organized into 1 armored brigade, 6 infantry brigades, 4 artillery regiments and supporting units.

PRINCIPAL EQUIPMENT
    <u>Weapons</u>:   Conventional
            60 Light and Medium Tanks (T-54, T-55, Charioteer, PT-76)
            75 Armored Personnel Carriers

NAVY

MANPOWER
    2,500 men

PRINCIPAL EQUIPMENT
    <u>Weapons</u>:   2 Corvettes
            3 Frigates
            1 Training Ship
            2 Minelayers
            15 Fast Patrol Boats
            5 Inshore Minesweepers
            12 Motor Patrol Boats
            4 Coast Guard Vessels
            10 Transport Craft
            7 Icebreakers

AIR FORCE

MANPOWER
    3,300 men

PRINCIPAL EQUIPMENT
    <u>Aircraft</u>:   Fighter-Bombers   30 MIG-21s
                                12 SAAB-35s
                                80 Fouga Magisters
                                30 SAAB-91s
            Helicopters   1 Bell 47Gs
                                2 Alouette IIs
                                3 Mi-4s
                                2 Mi-8s
            Transports   8 C-47s
                                2 Pembrokes
                                2 Il-28s
    <u>Missiles</u>:   Atoll
            Sidewinder

BASES
    Utti, Pori, Kupio, Kauhava, Jyvaskla, Rovaniemi, Tampere, Halli.

MISCELLANEOUS DATA

DEFENSE AGREEMENTS
    Changes in size of forces must be approved by UN Security Council.
INTERNAL SECURITY FORCES
    6,000 men
CONSCRIPTION LAW
    Compulsory service for all males to age 60; 4 month conscript training begins at age 17.
NATIONAL FLAG
    Extended blue cross on a white field.
OFFICIAL LANGUAGE
    Finnish
COMBAT EFFECTIVENESS
    Limited
SPECIAL NOTES
    Finland is an active member in many international bodies. However, due to proximity to Soviet Union, maintains a low posture in defense matters.

FRANCE

Defense Budget $ 12,250,000,000
Population   53,586,000
Manpower in the Armed Forces   505,000
Defense as % of GNP   4.6%

ARMY

MANPOWER
    330,000 men (Reserves of 450,000)

GENERAL
    Organized into 5 mechanized division, 1 airborne division, 1 air-portable brigade, 2 Alpine brigades, 2 motorized infantry regiments, 4 armored car regiments, 1 parachute battalion, 25 infantry battalions.

Overseas Committments:		
	Germany	60,000
	Afars and Issas	2,000
	Malagasy	1,250
	Chad	2,500
	Gabon	400
	Ivory Coast	600
	Senegal	1,450
	Berlin	2,000
	Reunion	4,000

PRINCIPAL EQUIPMENT

  Weapons: 1100 AMX-30 Medium Tanks
             1120 AMX-13 Light Tanks
              720 Armored Cars
              600+ Armored Personnel Carriers

  Missiles: Honest John
             Hawk
             Roland
             Pluton
             Nord SS-11
             Entac
             Milan

  Aircraft: 400+ Helicopters (Bell, Alouette, Puma, Gazelle)
             300 Liaison Light Aircraft

NAVY

MANPOWER
    69,000 men (Reserves of 90,000)

PRINCIPAL EQUIPMENT

  Vessels: 2 Aircraft Carriers
             2 Cruisers
             2 Guided Missile Frigates
            20 Destroyers
            25 Frigates
            11 Submarines
             5 Corvettes
            70 Minesweepers
             9 Survey Vessels
            15 Patrol Craft

		24 Motor Launches
		7 Landing Ships
		10 Landing Craft
		5 Depot Ships
		7 Oilers
		5 Transports
		13 Boom Defense Vessels
		3 Sailing Training Vessels
		15 Inshore Minesweepers
		1 Helicopter Carrier
		1 Command Ship
Aircraft:	ASW Patrol	60 Breguet Alizes
		38 Breguet Atlantiques
	Reconnaissance	12 Entenards
		20 P-2 Neptunes
	Fighters	36 Entenards
	Interceptors	38 F-8Es
	Helicopters	44 H-34s
		50 Alouettes
		16 Super Frelons
Missiles:	Exocet	
	Masurca	
	Malafon	
	Tartar	
	Martel	
	Matra	
	Sidewinder	

AIR CRAFT

MANPOWER
 106,000 men (Reserves of 50,000)

PRINCIPAL EQUIPMENT

Aircraft:	Air Defense:	
	Interceptors	45 Mirage IIIs
		45 Mirage F-1s
		45 Super Mystere B-2s
	Tactical Air	120 Mirage IIIs
		30 Mirage Vs
		55 F-100s
		75 Jaguar
		45 Mirage IIIRs
	Transport	50 Transall C-160s
		150 Nord Noratlas'
		4 DC-6s
		3 DC-8s
	Helicopters	93 H-34s
		80 Alouette II/IIIs
Missiles:	Nike Ajax	
	Nike Hercules	
	Nord AS-20	
	Nord AS-30	
	Matra	
	Nord 5210	
	Martel	

FRANCE

BASES
Toulouse-Francazal, Digon-Longvic, Cambrai-Epinoy, Dugny-Le Dourget, Bordeaux-Merignac, Villacoublay, Creil, Reims, St. Dizier, Orange-Caritat, Luxeuil, Mont-de-Marsan, Pau, Cazaux, Chatres, Orleans-Bricy, Istres, Evreux, Solenzara, Metz-Frascati, Strasbourg, Colmar, Nancy-Ochey, Toul-Rosieres, Tananarive-Ivato, Djibouti, Bretigny, Amberieu, Fort Lamy, Salon-de-Province, Avord, Tours, Cognac, Caen-Carpiquet, Chambery, Aulnat, Papeete, Hao, Aix, Berlin-Tegel.

FRENCH STRATEGIC FORCES

4 Ballistic Missile Submarines with 16 MSBS M-1 Missiles
2 Land-based Squadrons, each with 9 IRBM's
54 Mirage IVA Bombers with nuclear capacity

MISCELLANEOUS DATA

DEFENSE AGREEMENTS
Although France withdrew from NATO, they adhere to the North Atlantic Council and participate in limited manner.
Defense agreements exist with many of previous French colonial states.

INTERNAL SECURITY FORCES
60,000 men

CONSCRIPTION LAW
Selective service for 12-15 months for males 18 to 50.

NATIONAL FLAG
A tri-color of blue, white and red vertical stripes.

OFFICIAL LANGUAGE
French

COMBAT EFFECTIVENESS
Excellent

SPECIAL NOTES
France is next to the United States and USSR as the largest exporter of arms to other countries. Sales to Arab states alone were:

Abu Dhabi	-	32 Mirage V Fighter-Bombers
	-	18 Mirage IIIEs
Iraq	-	40 Alouette Helicopters
Libya	-	40 Mirage F-1s
Saudi Arabia	-	38 Mirage IIIs
		450 AMX-10 and AMX-30 Tanks
		Crotale SAM Missiles
Syria	-	50 Super Frelon Helicopters
Egypt	-	64 Mirage F-1s
		38 Mirage IIIs
		42 Gazelle Helicopters

Defense Budget	$ 10,000,000
Population	510,000
Manpower in the Armed Forces	1,350
Defense as % of GNP	3.5%

ARMY

MANPOWER
    700 men
GENERAL
    Organized into 2 infantry battalions.
PRINCIPAL EQUIPMENT
    <u>Weapons</u>: Conventional
                  Armored Cars
    <u>Vessels</u>: 2 Harbor Patrol Boats

NAVY

  None.

AIR FORCE

MANPOWER
    75 men
PRINCIPAL EQUIPMENT
    <u>Aircraft</u>: 2 Broussard Transports
                  1 C-47
                  2 Liaison Aircraft
                  1 Helicopters
BASES
    Libreville and Port Gentil.

MISCELLANEOUS DATA

DEFENSE AGREEMENTS
    Equatorial Defense Council, Union Africaine et Malgache, France.
MAP TYPE ASSISTANCE RECEIVED FROM
    France
INTERNAL SECURITY FORCES
    600 man Gendarmerie (considered part of Armed Forces)
CONSCRIPTION LAW
    Volunteer forces
NATIONAL FLAG
    Green, yellow and blue horizontal stripes.
OFFICIAL LANGUAGE
    French
COMBAT EFFECTIVENESS
    Negligible

GERMANY, EAST

Defense Budget	$2,540,000,000
Population	17,068,318
Manpower in the Armed Forces	194,000
Defense as % of GNP	6%

DEFENSE ESTABLISHMENT

Under the Minister of Defense are five deputy ministers and two deputy chiefs. Four of the deputies served jointly as chiefs of the major administrations of the rear services, training, political administration, and of the main staff. The chiefs of the naval, border, air and air defense forces, as well as a number of more important support administrations and departments are also included within the minister's staff, but not at the deputy level.

The minister has retained direct control over the ground forces, delegating much of the detail work to the chief of the main staff, and there is no ground force commander equivalent to those of the naval and air forces. Top area and tactical commanders are responsible directly to the minister and to the chief of the main staff. The main staff also controls several administrations that have functions common to all service elements.

ARMY

MANPOWER
100,000 men (Reserves of 200,000)

GENERAL
Organized into 2 military districts: Southern and Northern (headquartered in Leipzig and Neubrandenburg, respectively).

Tactical organization consists of 6 army divisions: 1 tank and two motorized infantry divisions are located in each district. Each division has regiments, battalions, companies, batteries and platoons.

Motorized divisions have 11,000 men; armored divisions 9,000.

Tank divisions have five regiments: three tank, one artillery, one motorized rifle. Typical tank divisions have 10 tank battalions with about 300 tanks motorized rifle divisions have 6 tank battalions with between 150 and 200 tanks.

All divisions have engineer, medical, communications, transportation, anti-aircraft, and one or more rocket battalions.

East German ground forces are equipped as well as or better than those in any other of the East European armies. All but light weapons are manufactured in the Soviet Union, and East Germany has a priority on tanks and artillery second only to the USSR.

Tank and motorized divisions are heavily equipped with other firepower, after the Soviet fashion, with about 25 percent of combat personnel being artillerymen.

PRINCIPAL EQUIPMENT
    Weapons: Tanks   Est. 1,800+ T-54, T-55, T-62s
                                         175 PT-76s
                  Vehicles
                            Est. 1,500+ Scout Cars and APC's
                  Artillery
                            Est. 850+ SU-100 Guns, 122/130
                                        152mm Guns
    Missiles: Frog
                  Scud B
    Anti-Tank & AA: Sagger
                            Snapper
                            Swatter
                            27/57/100mm AA Guns

NAVY

MANPOWER
    16,000 men   (Reserves of 30,000)
GENERAL
    Organized into three flotillas, based at Baltic ports of Peenmunde, Warnemunde and Sassnitz. The main naval headquarters is Rostok with schools and training facilities at Stralsund.
    The border troops also have a brigade-sized naval force for coast guard type duties. Although a part of the border troop organization, they are supported by, and are subject to some control by the Navy.

PRINCIPAL EQUIPMENT
    Vessels: Over 400 ships of a wide range of types, but all small and with limited range. Largest vessels are under 1000 tons displacement.

                      2 Escorts
                    24 Coastal Escorts
                    20 Submarine Chasers
                    12 Missile Patrol Boats
                    38 Inshore Minesweepers
                    14 Coastal Minesweepers
                    70 Motor Torpedo Boats
                    20 Landing Craft
    Aircraft: 16 Mi-4 Helicopters
    Missiles: Styx

AIR FORCE

MANPOWER
    25,000 men (Reserves of 30,000)
GENERAL
    Equipped almost exclusively for air defense and support of ground forces. Fighter-bomber aircraft have the only offensive capability. Surface-to-air missile and anti-aircraft units that are not within the Army are subordinate to the Air Force and Air Defense Command.

GERMANY, EAST 79

Tactical organization consists of two air divisions-
one ground support and one interceptor, plus a number
of anti-aircraft artillery and SAM regiments.

BASES
Tutow, Marxalde, Drewitz, Cottbus, Jocksdorf, Kamenz, Bautzen, Klotsche, Rechlin, Oranienburg, Schoenwalde, Staaken, Werder, Leipzig, Weimar, Neubrandenburg, Peenemunde, Rothenburg, Dessau, Strausberg.

PRINCIPAL EQUIPMENT
  Aircraft: Fighter/
                Interceptors   300+ MiG-21/23s
              Fighter-Bombers   15   Su-7s
                                   40   MiG-17s
              Transports   40+ An-2/14/24s
                                        Il-14/18s
              Helicopters   28   Mi-4s
                                    4   Mi-8s
                                    5   Mi-24s
                                    3   Mi-1s
                                    6   Mi-2s

  Missiles: Guideline
              Atoll
              Alkali

BORDER TROOPS

MANPOWER
    53,000 men
GENERAL
    Operate as branch of the Army rather than as part of Internal Security Forces as in other communist states. The basic tactical unit is the brigade with 3 regiments. (Regiments are smaller than Army counterpart). In peacetime, they provide border patrol; in war time, they serve as infantry and fall back for holding duties.
PRINCIPAL EQUIPMENT
    Light Weapons
    Armored Vehicles

MISCELLANEOUS DATA

DEFENSE AGREEMENTS
    U.S.S.R., Warsaw Pact
MAP TYPE ASSISTANCE RECEIVED FROM
    U.S.S.R.
INTERNAL SECURITY FORCES
    17,000 Security Troops
    400,000 People's Militia
CONSCRIPTION LAW
    All males 18 to 50 liable for service of 18 months in Army or 2 years in Navy and Air Force.
MILITARY SCHOOLS
    Ernst, Thallmann Academy (Army)
    Karl Liebknecht Academy (Navy)
    Franz Mehring Academy (Air Force)

Rosa Luxembourg School (Border Guards)
Friedrich Engels Military Academy (Political)
Variety of Service and Training Schools

NATIONAL FLAG

Tri-color of black, red and gold horizontal stripes over which the coat of arms is super-imposed.

OFFICIAL LANGUAGE

German

COMBAT EFFECTIVENESS

East German military forces must be ranked as one of the most proficient in Europe and second only to Soviet Forces amongst all Warsaw Pact countries.

SPECIAL NOTES

Soviet Forces in East Germany are the strongest concentration of Soviet units outside the USSR - 20 divisions of which 10 are tank divisions, with over 7,500 tanks (about 30% of total Soviet tank inventory).

There are over 300,000 ground troops with about 25,000 Air Force personnel.

Tactical aviation units supporting or providing air defense for Soviet Forces have over 700 interceptors and fighter-bombers and about 300 transports.

Operation of the early warning and air defense system along the West German border is a joint Soviet-East German effort.

GERMANY, FED. REP. OF

Defense Budget	$ 12,029,000,000
Population	63,671,000
Manpower in the Armed Forces	490,000
Defense as % of GNP	5.0%

ARMY

MANPOWER
  340,000 men (Plus 35,000 Territorial Force and 525,000 Reservists)

GENERAL
  Organized into 12 armored, 12 armored infantry, 3 motorized infantry, 2 mountain, 2 airborne brigades, and 3 missile groups.

PRINCIPAL EQUIPMENT
  Weapons:
    1,500 M-48 Tanks
    2,300 Leopard Tanks
    9,000 Armored Personnel Carriers
    1,100 Tank Destroyers
      900 Pieces of Heavy Artillery
       50 SP AA Guns
  Aircraft: 12 Dornier Liaison
    Helicopters   50 Bell 47s
                    20 Vertol H-21s
                   115 CH-53s
                   340 Alouette's
                   230 Bell UH-1s
  Missiles: Honest John
             Sergeant
             SS-11 AT
             TOW AT
             Redeye
             Cobra
             Nord AS-20

NAVY

MANPOWER
  39,000 men (Includes Naval Aviation)

GENERAL
  One of the largest fleets in Europe operating out of four bases.

PRINCIPAL EQUIPMENT
  Vessels: 11 Destroyers
              8 Frigates
             13 Submarines
              5 Corvettes
             13 Escort and Support Ships
             24 Coastal Minesweepers
             30 Inshore Minesweepers
             10 Patrol Vessels
             23 Patrol Boats
             40 MTBs
             24 Landing Ships
             30 Fast Minesweepers
             44 Miscellaneous Vessels

Aircraft: 120 F-104s
            20 Breguet Atlantiques ASW
            20 Sikorsky S-53 Helicopters
            30 Westland Helicopters
            20 Do-28s Utility Aircraft
            15 Lockheed S-3ASW
Missiles: Tartar
            Sidewinder
            Standard
            Nord AS-12
            Kormoran
            Exocet
            Seacat

AIR FORCE

MANPOWER
    110,000 men (Reserves of 85,000)
PRINCIPAL EQUIPMENT
    Aircraft: Fighter-Bombers   175 F-4Fs
                                   250 F-104s
                                   290 Fiat G-91Rs
                Reconnaissance   85 RF-4Es
                Transports   88 Transall C-160s
                                     4 Boeing 707s
                                   100 Do-28Ds
                                     3 Jetstars
                                    12 MBB 320s
                Helicopters   10 Alouette IIs
                                   120 Bell UH-1Ds
    Missiles: Hawk
                Nike Hercules
                Pershing
                Sidewinder
                Sparrow
                AS-20
                Roland
BASES
    Norvenich, Lechfeld, Buchel, Memmingen, Diepholz, Rheine-Hopsten, Husum, Kaufbeuren Lowenthal, Sylt, Pferdsfel, Oldenburg, Leipheim, Wittmundhafen, Leck, Bremgarten, Neubiberg, Ahlhorn, Hohn, Landsberg, Koln/Wahn, Jever, Furstenfeldbruck, Uetersen, Wunstorf, Fassberg, Manching, Oberpfaffenhofen, Erding, Ingolstadt, Giebelstadt.

MISCELLANEOUS DATA

DEFENSE AGREEMENTS
    NATO
MAP TYPE ASSISTANCE RECEIVED FROM
    U.S.
INTERNAL SECURITY FORCES
    30,000 men

GERMANY, FED. REP. OF

CONSCRIPTION LAW
    Compulsory service for 18 months.
NATIONAL FLAG
    Black, red and gold horizontal stripes.
OFFICIAL LANGUAGE
    German
COMBAT EFFECTIVENESS
    Excellent
SPECIAL NOTES
    On order - 210 Panavia 200 aircraft; 200 Breguet-
  Dassault/Dornier Alpha jets.

Defense Budget	$ 50,000,000
Population	8,559,313
Manpower in the Armed Forces	16,600
Defense as % of GNP	3.0%

DEFENSE ESTABLISHMENT

The Minister of Defense directs the administration and activities of the military establishment. He is advised by the Armed Forces Council, which serves to coordinate the interests of the top civilian and military levels of control.

The Armed Forces Council advises the cabinet on all major matters of policy relating to defense and military strategy, including the role of the armed forces, military budgets, administration, and the promotion of all officers above the rank of lieutenant colonel or its equivalent. Although the president appoints senior officers to major military command positions, his designations must be approved by the council.

ARMY

MANPOWER
   14,000 men
GENERAL
   The Army is commanded by a general officer with headquarters in Accra. The staff is organized along British lines. The components of the Army are divided into field forces for combat, which operates under a tactical chain of command, and the supporting units and installations, which were controlled directly by Army headquarters through staff directorates.

   Field forces are organized into six infantry battalions, one recon and one engineer battalion, one paratroop battalion.

   Battalion cantonments are widely dispersed through the country at Accra, Takoradi, Tema, Ho, Pong-Tamale, Tamale, Sunyani, Dunkwa, and Golokuati.
PRINCIPAL EQUIPMENT
   Weapons: Saladin and Ferret Armored Cars
              Light Weapons - Small Arms, Rifles,
              Machine Guns and Mortars.

NAVY

MANPOWER
   1,100 men
GENERAL
   The Navy's mission is to patrol the coastal regions to control smuggling and to prevent violation of other maritime laws, and air-sea rescue operations.

GHANA

PRINCIPAL EQUIPMENT
    Vessels: 2 Corvettes
                   1 Coastal Minesweeper
                   2 Inshore Minesweepers
                   2 Seaward Defense Boats
                   3 Patrol Boats
                   1 Repair Vessel
                   2 Landing Craft

AIR FORCE

MANPOWER
    1,500 men
GENERAL
    Primary mission is to provide close support for the Army. It also provides medical evacuation, aerial survey, photographic missions, and similar work for civilian authorities. They also inspect power lines and conduct aerial spraying plus assist in air-sea rescue operations.
PRINCIPAL EQUIPMENT
    Aircraft: Transports   8 BN Islanders
                                        6 Skyvans
                                        6 F-27s
                                        3 H.S. Herons
                                        1 H.S. 125
                 Armed Trainers   5 Aeromacchi 326s
                                        6 S.A. Bulldogs
                 Helicopters   5 Alouette IIIS
                                        3 Hughes 300s
                                        2 Bell 212s
                                        3 Sikorsky H-19s
BASES
    Takoradi, Accra, Tamale, and remote airstrips.

MISCELLANEOUS DATA

DEFENSE AGREEMENTS
    OAU
MAP TYPE ASSISTANCE RECEIVED FROM
    Australia, Canada, Israel, India, New Zeland, Pakistan, U.S., U.K., U.S.S.R., Yugoslavia.
INTERNAL SECURITY FORCES
    3,500 Worker's Brigade
CONSCRIPTION LAW
    Volunteer forces
MILITARY SCHOOLS
    Ghana Military Academy, Armed Forces Training Center
NATIONAL FLAG
    Tri-color in horizontal red, yellow and green stripes, with a five-pointed black star in the center.
OFFICIAL LANGUAGE
    English
COMBAT EFFECTIVENESS
    Limited

Defense Budget	$ 675,000,000
Population	9,073,000
Manpower in the Armed Forces	150,000
Defense as % of GNP	6.9%

ARMY

MANPOWER
   120,000 men (Reserves of 350,000)

GENERAL
   Organized into 11 infantry, 1 armored divisions; 1 commando brigade, 3 missile battalions.

PRINCIPAL EQUIPMENT
   Weapons: Conventional
              300 M-47 Tanks
              500 M-48 Tanks
              190 AMX-30 Tanks
              Armored Cars
              Armored Personnel Carriers
              Light and Heavy Artillery
   Aircraft: 65 Piper and Cessna Liaison
              15 Bell 47s
               2 NAR Commanders
   Missiles: Honest John
              Hawk

NAVY

MANPOWER
   17,800 Men (Reserves of 50,000)

PRINCIPAL EQUIPMENT
   Vessels: 9 Destroyers
               4 Frigates
               7 Submarines
               8 Patrol Vessels (with Exocet)
               5 Escort Minesweepers
              14 Coastal Minesweepers
               2 Coastal Minelayers
               2 Survey Ships
               6 Motor Launchers
               1 Repair Ship
              12 Motor Torpedo Boats
              14 Landing Ships
               2 Depot Ships
               1 Salvage Vessel
               7 Water Carriers
               3 Lighthouse Tenders
   Missiles: Exocet

AIR FORCE

MANPOWER
   23,000 men (Reserves of 30,000)

GREECE

PRINCIPAL EQUIPMENT

Aircraft:	ASW Patrol	8 HU-16s
	Fighter-Bombers	40 F-104s
		14 F-4s
		75 F-5s
		60 F-84s
		60 A-7Ds
		40 Mirage F1s
	Interceptors	40 F-5s
		16 F-102s
	Reconnaissance	14 RF-5s
		18 F-84Fs
	Helicopters	10 Bell 47s
		10 UH-19s
		8 Alouette IIs
		6 Bell 206s
	Transports	35 C-47s
		40 Noratlas
		18 C-130s

Missiles: Sidewinder
Nike Ajax
Nike Hercules

BASES
Tanagra, Araxos, Nea Ankhialos, Soudha Bay, Andravidha, Larissa, Elevsis, Tatoi, Dhekelia, Kalamai, Timbakion, Megara.

MISCELLANEOUS DATA

DEFENSE AGREEMENTS
NATO, Balkan Alliance
MAP TYPE ASSISTANCE RECEIVED FROM
U.S.
INTERNAL SECURITY FORCES
30,000 men
CONSCRIPTION LAW
24 months' compulsory service at 21; 29 years in reserves.
NATIONAL FLAG
5 blue horizontal stripes alternating with 4 white ones, and a white cross superimposed on a blue background in the upper left hand corner.
OFFICIAL LANGUAGE
Greek
COMBAT EFFECTIVENESS
Excellent
SPECIAL NOTES
Greece withdrew its forces from NATO during the 1974 crisis with Turkey over Cyprus.

GUATEMALA

Defense Budget $ 21,000,000
Population 6,064,269
Manpower in the Armed Forces 8,985
Defense as % of GNP 1.5%

ARMY

MANPOWER
7,800 men

GENERAL
Organized into 6 infantry battalions, 1 armored cavalry troop, 2 artillery battalions, engineer, parachute, and medical battalions.

PRINCIPAL EQUIPMENT
Weapons: Conventional
15 M-3, M-4 Tanks
18 M-8 Armored Cars
10 M-113 Armored Personnel Carriers
30 Howitzers (105mm)

NAVY

MANPOWER
185 men (1 Marine Company)

PRINCIPAL EQUIPMENT
Vessels: 1 Gunboat
4 Coast Guard Vessels
1 Rescue Boat

AIR FORCE

MANPOWER
1,000 men

PRINCIPAL EQUIPMENT
Aircraft: Light Bombers   3 B-26s
Fighter-Bombers 6 F-51s
                 8 A-37Bs
Transports   4 C-47s
                 1 C-54
Helicopters   6 UH-12Bs
                 3 Sikorsky S-55s
                 2 UH-1Bs

BASES
La Aurora, Puerto Barrios, Los Cipresales, San Jose, Retal Muleu.

MISCELLANEOUS DATA

DEFENSE AGREEMENTS
Rio Pact

MAP TYPE ASSISTANCE RECEIVED FROM
U.S.

GUATEMALA

INTERNAL SECURITY FORCES
    4,500 men
CONSCRIPTION LAW
    2 years' compulsory service, but not universal for all males 18 to 50.
NATIONAL FLAG
    Blue, white and blue vertical bands, with national coat of arms centered on white band.
OFFICIAL LANGUAGE
    Spanish
COMBAT EFFECTIVENESS
    Limited
SPECIAL NOTES
    Dispute over Beliz created situation in 1975 in which Britain dispatched military reinforcements into area as Guatemala was reported to be massing troops on border.

Defense Budget	$ 21,000,000
Population	4,500,000
Manpower in the Armed Forces	5,300
Defense as % of GNP	4.2%

ARMY

MANPOWER
 4,800 men (Plus Militia of 3,000)

GENERAL
 Organized into 5 infantry, 1 artillery and 3 engineer battalions.

PRINCIPAL EQUIPMENT
 Weapons: 20 T-34 Tanks
           20 Armored Personnel Carriers
           Light and Heavy Artillery

NAVY

MANPOWER
 200 men

PRINCIPAL EQUIPMENT
 Vessels: 6 Motor Torpedo Boats
           2 Patrol Boats
           4 Motor Gunboats

AIR FORCE

MANPOWER
 300 men

PRINCIPAL EQUIPMENT
 Aircraft: Fighter-Bombers   8 MIG-17s
                              3 MIG-21s
                              3 MIG-21s
            Transports   2 Il-18s
                              4 Il-14s
                              4 An-14s
            Helicopters   2 Bell 47Gs
                              5 Alouette II/IIIs
                              3 Pumas

BASES
 Conakry, Boke, Kankan, Kissidougou, N'Zerekore

MISCELLANEOUS DATA

DEFENSE AGREEMENTS
 OAU

MAP TYPE ASSISTANCE RECEIVED FROM
 U.K., West Germany, U.S.S.R.

INTERNAL SECURITY FORCE
 3,300 men

GUINEA

CONSCRIPTION LAW
    Compulsory service for 2 years.
NATIONAL FLAG
    Red, yellow and green vertical stripes.
OFFICIAL LANGUAGE
    French
COMBAT EFFECTIVENESS
    Limited
SPECIAL NOTES
    Soviets have established naval and air base facilities in Guinea.

Defense Budget	$ 4,000,000
Population	828,000
Manpower in the Armed Forces	1,400
Defense as % of GNP	2.0%

ARMY

MANPOWER
   1,300 men
GENERAL
   Composed of 2 infantry battalions and women's army corps unit.
PRINCIPAL EQUIPMENT
   Weapons: Conventional
              Armored Cars
              Mortars

NAVY

MANPOWER
   50 men
PRINCIPAL EQUIPMENT
   Vessels: 3 Patrol Boats

AIR FORCE

MANPOWER
   50 men
GENERAL
   Operates as part of the Army.
PRINCIPAL EQUIPMENT
   Aircraft: 2 Helio 269 Helicopters
              3 BN-2 Transports

MISCELLANEOUS DATA

DEFENSE AGREEMENTS
   U.K.
MAP TYPE ASSISTANCE RECEIVED FROM
   U.K.
INTERNAL SECURITY FORCES
   2,200 men
CONSCRIPTION LAW
   Volunteer forces.
NATIONAL FLAG
   A green field with a black-edged red triangle superimposed on a white-edged yellow triangle.
OFFICIAL LANGUAGE
   English
COMBAT EFFECTIVENESS
   Limited.

HAITI

```
Defense Budget              $ 8,000,000
Population                    5,512,000
Manpower in the Armed Forces      5,500
Defense as % of GNP                1.0%
```

ARMY

MANPOWER
 5,000 men (Plus 10,000 Militia)
GENERAL
 Organized into combat teams and Presidental Guard.
PRINCIPAL EQUIPMENT
 <u>Weapons</u>: Light Artillery
                 9 Light Tanks
                 Armored Cars
                 Armored Personnel Carriers

NAVY

MANPOWER
 250 men
PRINCIPAL EQUIPMENT
 <u>Vessels</u>: 5 Small Patrol Boats
                 1 Tank Landing Craft

AIR FORCE

MANPOWER
 250 men
PRINCIPAL EQUIPMENT
 <u>Aircraft</u>: 6 F-51s
                  2 C-45s
                  3 C-47s
                  2 Cessna 310s
                  6 Helicopters

MISCELLANEOUS DATA

DEFENSE AGREEMENTS
 Rio Pact
MAP TYPE ASSISTANCE RECEIVED FROM
 U.S.
INTERNAL SECURITY FORCES
 12,500 men
CONSCRIPTION LAW
 Volunteer forces
NATIONAL FLAG
 Black and red vertical halves, with a white rectangular panel in the center bearing the national coat of arms.
OFFICIAL LANGUAGE
 French
COMBAT EFFECTIVENESS
 Limited.

Defense Budget	$ 16,000,000
Population	3,036,000
Manpower in the Armed Forces	6,400
Defense as % of GNP	3.7%

ARMY

MANPOWER
  5,000 men
GENERAL
  Organized into 3 infantry battalions, 20 infantry companies, 2 artillery brigades and support units.
PRINCIPAL EQUIPMENT
  <u>Weapons</u>:   Light Artillery
              17 Light Tanks
              Armored Personnel Carriers
              Armored Cars

NAVY

MANPOWER
  200 men
PRINCIPAL EQUIPMENT
  <u>Vessels</u>:   8 Coast Guard Craft

AIR FORCE

MANPOWER
  1,200 men
PRINCIPAL EQUIPMENT
  <u>Aircraft</u>:   12 F-4s
                5 F-51s
                3 C-47s
                1 C-54
                4 Cessna 180s
                3 H-19 Helicopters

MISCELLANEOUS DATA

DEFENSE AGREEMENTS
  Rio Pact
MAP TYPE ASSISTANCE RECEIVED FROM
  U.S.
INTERNAL SECURITY FORCES
  2,500 men
CONSCRIPTION LAW
  Volunteer forces.
NATIONAL FLAG
  Two blue horizontal stripes separated by a white stripe bearing a cluster of five blue stars.
OFFICIAL LANGUAGE
  Spanish
COMBAT EFFECTIVENESS
  Limited

HUNGARY

Defense Budget $484,000,000
Population 10,523,000
Manpower in the Armed Forces 109,000
Defense as % of GNP 3.2%

ARMY

MANPOWER
 95,000 men (Reserves of 125,000)
GENERAL
 Comprises 2 tank, 4 motorized rifle divisions; 1 airborne regiment.
PRINCIPAL EQUIPMENT
 Weapons: 1500+ T-54/T-55 Tanks
           100+ T-34 Tanks
           150   PT-76 Tanks
           1500 Armored Scout Cars
           400   Armored Personnel Carriers
           400   Pieces Heavy Artillery
 Missiles: Frog
           Scud
           Guideline
           Snapper
           Sagger
           Swatter

NAVY

The Navy has been dissolved and its 1,500 men operate with police for river patrol duties. They have 30 patrol boats.

AIR FORCE

MANPOWER
 13,000 men (Reserves of 15,000)
PRINCIPAL EQUIPMENT
 Aircraft: Bombers   12 IL-28s
           Fighter-Bombers 36 MIG-19s
                           36 MIG-21s
                           24 MIG-17s
                           12 Su-7s
           Helicopters   30 Mi-1/4/8s
           Transports   10 An-2s
                           10 Il-14s
                           6 Li-2s
 Missiles: Atoll
           Guideline
BASES
 Budapest, Miskolc, Pecs, Debrecen, Kiskunfelegyhaza, Nyiregyhaza, Estergom, Szolnok, Kaposvar, Szeged, Dombova, Tokol, Gyor, Papa, Szombathely, Szekesfehervar.

MISCELLANEOUS DATA

DEFENSE AGREEMENTS
    Warsaw Pact
MAP TYPE ASSISTANCE RECEIVED FROM
    U.S.S.R.
INTERNAL SECURITY FORCES
    35,000 men
    150,000 People's Militia
CONSCRIPTION LAW
    2 years' compulsory service for all males age 18.
NATIONAL FLAG
    Red, white and green horizontal stripes.
OFFICIAL LANGUAGE
    Hungarian
COMBAT EFFECTIVENESS
    Excellent
SPECIAL NOTES
    Four Soviet divisions (2 tank) are stationed in Hungary.

INDIA

Defense Budget	$ 2,261,000,000
Population	614,962,000
Manpower in the Armed Forces	941,000
Defense as % of GNP	5.2%

ARMY

MANPOWER
  825,000 men (50,000 Territorial Army)

GENERAL
  Comprises 4 commands with 25 divisions; 13 infantry, 10 mountain, 2 armored, plus 2 paratroop brigades and support units.

PRINCIPAL EQUIPMENT
  Weapons: 200 Centurion Tanks
             1000 T-54/T-55 Tanks
             400 Vijayanta Tanks
             225 M-4 Tanks
              25 M-47 Tanks
             150 AMX-13 Light Tanks
             150 PTO76 Tanks
             Armored Personnel Carriers
             3000+ Light and Heavy Artillery Pieces
  Missiles: Entac
             SS-11
             Tigercat
  Aircraft: 60 Krishak Liaison
              15 Auster AOPs

NAVY

MANPOWER
  36,000 men

PRINCIPAL EQUIPMENT
  Vessels: 1 Aircraft Carrier
             6 Submarines
             2 Cruisers
             2 Destroyers
            20 Destroyer Escorts
             8 Fast Patrol Boats with Styx SSM
             7 Patrol Craft
             6 Motor Torpedo Boats
             1 Submarine Tender
             4 Coastal Minesweepers
             2 Inshore Minesweepers
             2 Seaward Defense Boats
             2 Tank Landing Ships
             2 Survey Vessels
             1 Repair Ship
             3 Small Oilers
            11 Auxiliaries
  Aircraft: 33 Sea Hawk Attack
            12 Alize Patrol/Recon
            14 Alouette III Helicopters
            12 Sea King Helicopters

AIR FORCE

MANPOWER
    80,000 men
PRINCIPAL EQUIPMENT
    Aircraft: Interceptors   180 Gnat F-1s
                                      300 MIG-21s
                Fighter-Bombers   75 Su-7s
                                      150 Hawker Hunters
                Bombers   50 Canberras
                Reconnaissance   8 Canberras
                Maritime-
                  Reconnaissance   6 L-1049 Connies
                Transports   34 An-12s
                                       55 C-119s
                                       70 HS-748s
                                       40 C-47s
                                       18 IL-14s
                                       30 DH Otters
                                       16 DH Caribous
                Helicopters   80 Mi-4s
                                       80 Alouette IIIs
                                       40 Mi-4s
                                       12 Bell 47s
                                      200 SA-315s
    Missiles: Atoll
                Guideline
                Tigercat
                AS-30 ASM
BASES
    Agartala, Uttarlad, Avatipur, Faridkot, Sirsawa, Ehuj, Jaisalmer, Okha, Palam, Kanpur, Bangalore, Srinagar, Amritsar, Ambala, Jodhpur, Jammu, Lucknow, Benarea, Gaya, Barrackpore, Bhopal, Hyderabad, Madras, Trivandrum, Begumpet, Coimbatore, Poona Adampur, Bikarnor, Chakeri, Gwalior, Halware, Jamnagar, Kalaikunda, Lalitpur, Pathankot, Jalahalli, Tambaram, Chandigarh, Agra, Sirsa, Bagdogra, Hasimara, Gorakhpur, Tozpur, Hindo, Bareilly, Bombay, Dum Dum, Panagarh, Jorhat, Kumbigran, Purnea.

MISCELLANEOUS DATA

DEFENSE AGREEMENTS

MAP TYPE ASSISTANCE RECEIVED FROM
    U.S., U.S.S.R.
INTERNAL SECURITY FORCES
    250,000 men
CONSCRIPTION LAW
    Volunteer Forces
NATIONAL FLAG
    Saffron, white and green horizontal stripes, with the 24-spoke Wheel of Asoka in blue on the white stripe.

INDIA

OFFICIAL LANGUAGE
    Hindi
COMBAT EFFECTIVENESS
    Excellent
SPECIAL NOTES
    India did not sign the Nuclear Non-Proliferation
Agreement and now has exploded its first nuclear
devices.

Defense Budget	$ 375,000,000
Population	133,714,000
Manpower in the Armed Forces	320,000
Defense as % of GNP	3.5%

ARMY

MANPOWER
    250,000 men (Plus 100,000 Militia)

GENERAL
    Composed of 16 territorial units; 8 armored battalions, 15 infantry brigades, 8 artillery regiments, and paracommando units.

PRINCIPAL EQUIPMENT
    <u>Weapons</u>:   160 Armored Cars
                    175 AMX-13, PT-76 Tanks
                    400 Armored Personnel Carriers
                    Light and Medium Artillery
                    Alouette Helicopters

NAVY

MANPOWER
    40,000 men (Including 14,000 Marines)

PRINCIPAL EQUIPMENT
    <u>Vessels</u>:   1 Cruiser
                    8 Destroyers
                    18 Submarine Chasers
                    7 Frigates
                    5 Submarines
                    3 Corvettes
                    5 Fleet Minesweepers
                    21 Motor Torpedo Boats
                    18 Motor Gunboats
                    9 Patrol Vessels
                    14 Coastal Minesweepers
                    25 Small Patrol Craft
                    9 Missile Boats (Styx)
                    8 Landing Ships
                    10 Landing Craft
                    2 Training Ships
                    2 Survey Vessels
                    4 Oilers
                    4 Transports
                    3 Depot Ships
    <u>Aircraft</u>:   24 MIG-19/MIG-21s
                    5 HU-16s ASW
                    20 Il-14 Bombers
                    12 S-55 Helicopters
                    4 S-58s
                    4 Mi-4s
                    3 Aero Commanders
    <u>Missiles</u>:   Styx

INDONESIA   101

AIR FORCE

MANPOWER
    30,000 men
PRINCIPAL EQUIPMENT
    Aircraft: Bombers   22 Tu-16s
                                 2 B-26s
                                 4 B-25s
                                10 IL-28s
                Fighters   16 F-86s
                                15 MIG-21s
                                40 MIG-17s
                                35 MIG-19s
                                12 F-51s
                Helicopters   12 Bell 204s
                                12 UH-34s
                                 8 Mi-6s
                                16 Mi-4s
                Transports   10 C-130s
                                 6 C-47s
                                 6 An-12s
                                 3 Jetstars
                                10 IL-14s
                                 9 DH Otters
                Liaison   11 Cessnas
    Missiles: Guideline
                Atoll
                Kennel

MISCELLANEOUS DATA

DEFENSE AGREEMENTS

MAP TYPE ASSISTANCE RECEIVED FROM
    U.S.S.R., Australia
INTERNAL SECURITY FORCES
    130,000 men
CONSCRIPTION LAW
    Emergency compulsory service.
NATIONAL FLAG
    A red horizontal stripe avove a white stripe.
OFFICIAL LANGUAGE
    Bahasa Indonesia
COMBAT EFFECTIVENESS
    Excellent
SPECIAL NOTES
    Indonesian troops entered East Timor in December, 1975 and refused to recognize UN order to withdraw its forces.

Defense Budget	$ 6,620,000,000
Population	30,000,000
Manpower in the ARmed Forces	253,000
Defense as % of GNP	N.A.

ARMY

MANPOWER
  175,000 men (Reserves of 300,000)

GENERAL
  Comprised of 3 armored divisions, 4 infantry divisions, 4 mixed brigades and 1 missile battalion.

PRINCIPAL EQUIPMENT
  Weapons: Light and Heavy Artillery
             Over 1,300 Tanks - Chieftain, M-47s, M-60s
             Over 2,000 Armored Personnel Carriers
  Aircraft: 74 Bell 205s
             36 Bell 206s
             20 CH-47s
             14 Kaman HH-43s
             45 Cessna 185s
             10 Cessna O-2s
              6 Cessna 310s
  Missiles: SS-11
             SS-12
             Hawk
             TOW

NAVY

MANPOWER
  13,000 men

GENERAL

PRINCIPAL EQUIPMENT
  Ships: 3 Destroyers
              4 Fast Frigates
              4 Corvettes
              4 Coastal Minesweepers
              2 Inshore Minesweepers
             16 Patrol Boats
             12 Hoovercraft
              4 Landing Craft
  Aircraft: 6 P-3A Orions
              4 Bell 205s
             14 Bell 206s
              6 Sikorsky SH-3s
              6 Bell 212s
              6 Aero Commanders
  Missiles: Seacat
             Sea Killer
             Tigercat

IRAN

AIR FORCE

MANPOWER
    65,000 men (Reserves of 18,000)
GENERAL
    Air Force became separate service in 1955 and is rapidly building up to the strongest in the Middle East.
PRINCIPAL EQUIPMENT

Aircraft:	Fighter-Bombers	230	F-4s
		98	F-5s
	Reconnaissance	16	RF-4s
		12	RF-5s
	Transports	56	C-130s
		6	Boeing 707s
		24	F-27s
		5	D.H. Beavers
	Helicopters	16	Super Frelons
		55	Bell 205s
		65	Bell 206s
		21	Bell 212s
		50	Vertol CH-47s
		10	Sikorsky SH-3Ds
Missiles:	SS-11		
	SS-12		
	Rapier		
	Hawk		
	Sparrow		
	Phoenix		
	Falcon		
	Sidewinder		
	Maverick		
	Tigercat		

MISCELLANEOUS DATA

DEFENSE AGREEMENTS
    CENTO
MAP TYPE ASSISTANCE RECEIVED FROM
    U.S., France
INTERNAL SECURITY FORCES
    50,000 men
CONSCRIPTION LAW
    2 years' compulsory service at age 21.
NATIONAL FLAG
    Green, white and red horizontal stripes, with a gold lion brandishing a sword, and a rising sun behind him, centered on the white stripe.
OFFICIAL LANGUAGE
    Persian, or Farisi, an Aryan language of the Indo-European group and written in Arabic characters.
COMBAT EFFECTIVENESS
    Excellent

SPECIAL NOTES

Iran remains with close ties to the Free World due to its 1,200 miles of open frontier facing the U.S.S.R.

Iran also remains close to Saudi Arabia with respect to future of new states in Persian Gulf area which might create a future threat to Iran's security.

Iran plans to acquire six fast patrol boats shortly from France.

Iran's Air Force is planning acquisition of almost 1,200 aircraft over the next four years.

Soviet pilots have been observed flying MiG-23s over Iran out of Iraqui bases.

Iran has expressed concern that a prospective rebellion in the Pakistani province of Baluchistan would give India an excuse for a Bangladesh type operation against Pakistan.

Over 2,000 Chieftain tanks on order.

IRAQ

Defense Budget	$ 825,000,000
Population	9,490,000
Manpower in the Armed Forces	102,000
Defense as % of GNP	10.0%

ARMY

MANPOWER
   90,000 men (Reserves of 250,000)

GENERAL
   Organized into 2 infantry, 2 mountain infantry, and one armored division; plus 1 brigade of Republican Guards.

PRINCIPAL EQUIPMENT
   Weapons: Over 1,035 Tanks (T-54, T-55, T-34, PT-76, M-24s)
              300 Armored Cars
              400+ Armored Personnel Carriers
              Light and Heavy Artillery (1300 Pieces)

NAVY

MANPOWER
   2,000 men

GENERAL
   Operates as integral part of the Army, the short coastline of Iraq in the Persian Gulf eliminates need for large component of Naval forces.

PRINCIPAL EQUIPMENT
   Ships: 12 Motor Torpedo Boats
             3 Submarine Chasers
             4 River Gunboats
             8 Harbor Patrol Boats
             4 River Launchers
             1 Lighthouse Tender
             1 Royal Yacht
             1 Tug

AIR FORCE

MANPOWER
   10,000 men (Reserves of 19,000)

GENERAL
   Operates as integral part of the Army, and provides air support for ground forces and air defense of country.

PRINCIPAL EQUIPMENT
   Aircraft: Bombers   8 Tu-16s
                                   12 Il-28s
               Fighter-Bombers   54 FGA-59 Hunters
                                   50 Su-7s and MiG-23s
               Interceptors   100 MiG-21s
                                   50 MiG-17s and 19s
               Reconnaissance   4 H.S. Hunters

Transports	10	An-2s
	2	Tu-124s
	13	Il-14s
	8	An-12s
	1	H.S. Heron
Helicopters	12	Alouette IIIs
	30	Mi-4s
	27	Mi-8s
	10	Mi-6s
	8	Wessex Mk-52s

<u>Missiles:</u> Guideline
Goa
Gainful
Strela
Atoll

MISCELLANEOUS DATA

DEFENSE AGREEMENTS
   Arab League Collective Security Pact, U.S.S.R.
MAP TYPE ASSISTANCE RECEIVED FROM
   U.K., U.S.S.R., Czechoslovakia
INTERNAL SECURITY FORCES
   18,000 men
CONSCRIPTION LAW
   2 years compulsory service for all males at age 18, with liability for service through age 40. 18 years in reserve.
MILITARY SCHOOLS
   Military College, Reserve College, Staff College, Air Force Flying College.
NATIONAL FLAG
   Red, white and black horizontal stripes, with three five-pointed green stars on the white stripe.
OFFICIAL LANGUAGE
   Arabic
COMBAT EFFECTIVENESS
   Excellent
SPECIAL NOTES
   Military coup in 1966 left government under military control which continues today.
   Nation racked by continued guerrilla warfare with Kurdish tribes in north of country.
   Iraq in constant power-play against Iran and Saudi Arabia over Persian Gulf area.
   Soviet pilots are flying Tu-16s and MiG-23s against Kurdish guerrillas for Iraq government.
   Flow of Soviet arms to Iraq has passed any potential needs for campaign against Kurds.
   Nation has $3-billion arms deal with U.S.S.R. providing among many items: hundreds of T-62 and T-64 tanks, batteries of Scud and Scalebird missiles, over 100 MIG-23, MIG-25s.

IRELAND

Defense Budget	$ 98,000,000
Population	3,086,990
Manpower in the Armed Forces	13,000
Defense as % of GNP	2.4%

ARMY

MANPOWER
  12,000 men (Plus 20,000 Reserves)
GENERAL
  Organized into 9 infantry battalions; 4 recon squadrons, 3 artillery units, 8 engineer companies.
PRINCIPAL EQUIPMENT
  Weapons: Conventional
             25 Armored Cars
             Light Artillery

NAVY

MANPOWER
  300 men
PRINCIPAL EQUIPMENT
  Vessels: 3 Corvettes
             2 Small Tenders

AIR FORCE

MANPOWER
  600 men
PRINCIPAL EQUIPMENT
  Aircraft: Fighter-Trainers   6 Super Magisters
             Transports   2 DH Doves
             Helicopters   8 Alouette IIIs
             Trainers   8 DH Chipmunks
                                8 Cessna 172s
                                4 BAC Provosts

MISCELLANEOUS DATA

DEFENSE AGREEMENTS
  U.K.
MAP TYPE ASSISTANCE RECEIVED FROM
  U.K.
INTERNAL SECURITY FORCES
  5,000 men
CONSCRIPTION LAW
  Volunteer forces

NATIONAL FLAG
   Green, white and orange vertical stripes.
OFFICIAL LANGUAGE
   Gaelic and English
COMBAT EFFECTIVENESS
   Limited
SPECIAL NOTES
   Country follows a consistent policy of non-alighment-maintaining strict neutrality.
   Irish troops have participated in UN peace-keeping roles in Cyprus, Lebanon, New Guinea, India, Pakistan and the Middle East.

ISRAEL

Defense Budget	$ 3,651,000,000
Population	3,000,000
Manpower in the Armed Forces	42,500 (300,000+ on Mobilization)
Defense as % of GNP	40%

ARMY

MANPOWER
   15,000 Regular (290,000 Reserves)
GENERAL
   Organized into brigades: 10 armored, 9 mechanized, 9 infantry, 5 parachute, 3 artillery.
PRINCIPAL EQUIPMENT
   <u>Weapons</u>:   Over 2,000 Tanks - (M-48, M-60, T-54, T-55, T-62, AMX-13, Centurions, PT-76)
   Over 2,300 Armored Personnel Carriers and Armored Cars
   Over 600 pieces of Light and Heavy Artillery
   <u>Missiles</u>:   LAW
   TOW
   Cobra
   SS-10
   SS-11
   Jericho

NAVY

MANPOWER
   3,300 men (4,000 Reserves)
GENERAL
   Small, but efficient.
PRINCIPAL EQUIPMENT
   <u>Ships</u>:   4 Submarines
   1 Destroyer
   1 Patrol Vessel
   9 Torpedo Boats
   16 Missile Boats
   8 Motor Launches
   12 Landing Craft
   2 High-speed Gunboats

AIR FORCE

MANPOWER
   14,000 men (Reserves of 20,000)
GENERAL
   The most proficient in the Middle East.
PRINCIPAL EQUIPMENT
   <u>Aircraft</u>:   Fighter-Bombers   200+ A-4Es
   140 F-4s
   47 Mirage IIIs
   30 Ouragans
   25 Mystere IVs

	Bombers	10	Vatours
	Fighters	30	Baraks
		20	Mystere B-2s
	Transports	30	Noratlas
		10	C-47s
		10	C-130s
		5	Boeing 707s
	Helicopters	20	Alouette IIIs
		12	Super Frelons
		18	Sikorsky CH-53s
		25	Bell 205s
		25	Bell UH-1Ds
	Liaison	40	Piper Super Cubs
		2	Pilatus Porter

<u>Missiles</u>: Matra
Hawk
Sparrow
Bullpup
AS-30
Shrike
Walleye
Maverick
Sidewinder
TOW
Shafrir

MISCELLANEOUS DATA

DEFENSE AGREEMENTS
    U.S.
MAP TYPE ASSISTANCE RECEIVED FROM
    U.S., U.S., France
INTERNAL SECURITY FORCES
    10,000 men
CONSCRIPTION LAW
    Men and single women 18 to 26 conscripted for 36 and 20 months respectively; a 2 year period for those 27-29; men and women in reserve until age 55 and 34 respectively.
NATIONAL FLAG
    A white field with a blue six-pointed Star of David bordered above and below by blue horizontal stripes.
OFFICIAL LANGUAGE
    Hebrew
COMBAT EFFECTIVENESS
    Excellent
SPECIAL NOTES
       In October 1973 War, which lasted 18 days, Israeli forces destroyed 415 aircraft, 2300 tanks, and close to 10,000 Arabs. Israeli casualties were about 2400 dead, 106 aircraft lost, and 600 tanks destroyed.
    The U.K. is selling 400 Centurion tanks to help fill this gap in tanks.
    The U.S. will supply 600 tanks and numerous F-4s and F-15s.
    Israel has replaced all losses incurred in the October War. Israel is now believed to have on hand approximately 10-15 nuclear weapons.

ITALY

Defense Budget	$ 4,100,000,000
Population	54,871,430
Manpower in the Armed Forces	420,000
Defense as % of GNP	3.0%

ARMY

MANPOWER
    300,000 men (Reserves of 700,000)

GENERAL
    Organized into 5 infantry and 2 armored divisions, 5 alpine brigades, 4 infantry brigades, 1 paratroop brigade, 1 cavalry brigade, 1 missile brigade, 4 missile battalions, and various support units.

PRINCIPAL EQUIPMENT

Weapons:
- 650 M-47 Tanks
- 500 Leopard Tanks
- 3000 M-113s Armored Personnel Carriers
- 700+ Artillery Pieces (105/155/175/203mm)

Aircraft:
- 100 SM.1019 Liaison
- 20 AM-3s
- 100+ Piper Liaison
- 30 Cessna O-1s
- 120 Bell 47s Helicopters
- 45 204s Helicopters
- 30 205s Helicopters
- 25 CH-47s Helicopters
- 90 206s Helicopters

Missiles:
- Lance
- Hawk
- Cobra AT
- TOW AT
- Mosquito AT

NAVY

MANPOWER
    41,000 men (Reserves of 140,000)

PRINCIPAL EQUIPMENT

Vessels:
- 2 Guided Missile Cruisers
- 4 Guided Missile Destroyers
- 7 Destroyers
- 11 Corvettes
- 3 Missile Patrol Boats
- 10 Motor Torpedo Boats
- 9 Submarines
- 37 Coastal Minesweepers
- 20 Inshore Minesweepers
- 1 Hydrofoil with Missiles
- 2 Landing Ships
- 40+ Miscellaneous Landing Craft
- 70+ Auxiliaries

Aircraft:
- 20 S-2 ASWs
- 24 SH-3 Helicopters

                    30 204 Helicopters
                    12 A-106 Helicopters
        Missiles: Terrier
                    Asroc
                    Standard
                    Tartar
                    Seakiller
                    Otomat
    Marine Force:
        2 Infantry Battalions

AIR FORCE

MANPOWER
    70,000 men (Reserves of 30,000)
PRINCIPAL EQUIPMENT
        Aircraft: Fighter-Bombers   150 F-104s
                                        75 G-91s
                    Reconnaissance   35 RF-104s
                                        14 Atlantiques
                    Transports   32 G-222s
                                        24 C-130s
                                         2 DC-9s
                                         2 DC-6s
                                        15 Vespa Jets
                    Helicopters   12 HU-16s
                                        15 AB-206s
                                        80 Bell 47s
        Missiles: Nike Hercules
                    Sparrow
                    Hawk
                    Sidewinder
                    Nord CT-20

MISCELLANEOUS DATA

DEFENSE AGREEMENTS
    NATO
MAP TYPE ASSISTANCE RECEIVED FROM
    U.S.
INTERNAL SECURITY FORCES
    76,000 men
CONSCRIPTION LAW
    National service of 18 months.
NATIONAL FLAG
    Green, white and red vertical stripes.
OFFICIAL LANGUAGE
    Italian
COMBAT EFFECTIVENESS
    Excellent

IVORY COAST

Defense Budget	$ 27,000,000
Population	4,700,000
Manpower in the Armed Forces	4,500
Defense as % of GNP	1.7%

DEFENSE ESTABLISHMENT

The Armed Forces are made up of four components - Army, Navy, Air Force and National Gendarmery.

The Army adopted a civil action program wherein its annual conscripts carry out public works projects of importance to the national economy.

The President has final authority in military matters and he coordinates his actions with the Council of Ministers. There is a Ministerial Defense Committee composed of the cabinet, and a military counterpart, the Superior Defense Council, made up of the Chief of Staff and the Inspector General of the Armed Forces and the Commandant of the National Gendarmery.

Under the President, who is Commander-in-Chief of the Armed Forces is the Minister of Defense.

ARMY

MANPOWER
   4,000 men
GENERAL
   Organized into three infantry battalions, one armored squadron, one parachute company, and two artillery battalions.
PRINCIPAL EQUIPMENT
   Weapons: Light Artillery
              10 AMX Light Tanks
              10 Armored Cars

NAVY

MANPOWER
   200 men
GENERAL
   Organized for coast guard type duties only.
PRINCIPAL EQUIPMENT
   Vessels: 3 Motor Gun Boats
              2 Landing Craft

AIR FORCE

MANPOWER
   300 men
GENERAL
   Small, with no combat aircraft per se.

PRINCIPAL EQUIPMENT
    <u>Aircraft:</u>   Transports   1 Grumman Gulfstream
                                        3 C-47s
                                          2 F-27s
                                          1 Dassault Falcon
                                          1 Aero Commander
                Liaison   7 MH Broussards
                Helicopter   5 Alouette II/IIIs
                                          1 SA-300
                                          3 Pumas

NATIONAL GENDARMERY

MANPOWER
    1,500 men
GENERAL
    Operates as national police, charged with public order and internal security.
PRINCIPAL EQUIPMENT
        Light Weapons
        Few Armored Cars

MISCELLANEOUS DATA

DEFENSE AGREEMENTS
    France, Niger, Union Africane et Malgache
MAP TYPE ASSISTANCE RECEIVED FROM
    France, Israel, U.S.
INTERNAL SECURITY FORCES
    3,000 men
CONSCRIPTION LAW
    Every male liable for service for 25 years, two of which must be on active duty and the balance in the reserves.
MILITARY SCHOOLS
    Military Preparatory School, Officers Trained Overseas.
NATIONAL FLAG
    Vertical tricolor of orange, white and green
OFFICIAL LANGUAGE
    French
COMBAT EFFECTIVENESS
    Limited

JAMAICA

Defense Budget	$ 8,000,000
Population	1,934,200
Manpower in the Armed Forces	1,000
Defense as % of GNP	0.6%

ARMY

MANPOWER
    1,000 men (Reserves of 1,000)
GENERAL
    Organized into 1 infantry battalion.
PRINCIPAL EQUIPMENT
    <u>Weapons</u>:   Conventional
                     Armored Cars

COAST GUARD

MANPOWER
    50 men
PRINCIPAL EQUIPMENT
    <u>Vessels</u>:   3 Patrol Craft

AIR WING

MANPOWER
    250 men
PRINCIPAL EQUIPMENT
    <u>Aircraft</u>:   2 Bell 57s Helicopters
                       2 Alouette II Helicopters
                       3 Light Aircraft

MISCELLANEOUS DATA

MAP TYPE ASSISTANCE RECEIVED FROM
    U.S.
INTERNAL SECURITY FORCES
    2,800 men
CONSCRIPTION LAW
    Volunteer forces
NATIONAL FLAG
    A gold diagonal cross or saltire, divides the flag into four triangles; the top and bottom triangles are green, and the remaining two black.
OFFICIAL LANGUAGE
    English
COMBAT EFFECTIVENESS
    Negligible

JAPAN

Defense Budget	$ 4,950,000,000
Population	110,950,000
Manpower in the Armed Forces	277,000
Defense as % of GNP	1.8%

ARMY

MANPOWER
 180,000 men (Reserves of 40,000)

GENERAL
 12 infantry divisions; 1 mechanized division, 1 airborne, 5 artillery, 5 engineer, 1 communications and 1 helicopter brigade.

PRINCIPAL EQUIPMENT

Weapons: 900 Tanks - Type 61, M-24, M-41s
500 Armored Personnel Carriers (Type 60, M-113, SU, SX)
Over 800 Light and Heavy Artillery Pieces

Missiles: Hawk
Nike-Hercules
Nike-Ajax
Honest John

Aircraft:
100+ Bell UH-1s Helicopters
125 Hughes 500s
 26 Sikorsky H-19s
 40 Vertol 107s
 75 Bell H-13s
100+ Cessna Liaison
 10 Mitsubishi MU-2Cs

NAVY

MANPOWER
 45,000 men (Reserves of 40,000)

PRINCIPAL EQUIPMENT

Vessels:
15 Submarines
 3 Helicopter Destroyers
 3 Guided Missile Destroyers
11 ASW Frigates
 5 Conventional Frigates
20 Sub Chasers
32 Coastal Minesweepers
11 Motor Torpedo Boats
40+ Landing Craft
 3 Depot Ships
 1 Oiler
 8 Auxiliaries
 2 Minelayers

Aircraft:
30 S-2A ASW Patrol
50 P-2H ASW Patrol
70 P-2J ASW Patrol
30 Shin Meiwa PS-1s ASW Patrol
 7 Transports R4Ds and YS-11s
10 Vertol KV-107s

JAPAN

                   12 Hughes OH-6s
                   40 Sikorsky SH-3s
                    6 Sikorsky S-61s
                  10 Sikorsky HSS-1s
                  43 Sikorsky HSS-2s
    <u>Missiles</u>:   Asroc
                  Tartar

<u>AIR FORCE</u>

MANPOWER
    45,000 men
PRINCIPAL EQUIPMENT
    <u>Aircraft</u>:   Fighters   150 F-4Es
                                     125 Mitsubishi FS
                                     200 F-104s
                Reconnaissance   18 RF4Es
                Transports   30 NAMC C1As
                                     13 YS-11s
                                   15 C-46s
                Helicopters   17 Vertol 107s
                                   25 Mitsubishi MU-2s
                                    8 Sikorsky S-62s
    <u>Missiles</u>: Nike Ajas and Hercules
                 Mitsubishi AAM-1
                 Sidewinder
BASES
    Matsushima, Chitose, Tachikawa, Hofu, Tsuiki, Manda, Hamamatsu, Miho, Miyazaki, Iruma, Komaki, Huakuri, Komatsu, Ashiya, Bofu, Gifu, Shizuhama, Yokota.

<u>MISCELLANEOUS DATA</u>

DEFENSE AGREEMENTS
    U.S.
MAP TYPE ASSISTANCE RECEIVED FROM
    U.S.
INTERNAL SECURITY FORCES
    100,000 men
CONSCRIPTION LAW
    Volunteer forces
NATIONAL FLAG
    A red sun with white field
OFFICIAL LANGUAGE
    Japanese
COMBAT EFFECTIVENESS
    Excellent
SPECIAL NOTES
    Japan, by treaty, is restricted to self-defense forces thus placing severe restrictions on types of equipment they can have in place.
    Defense budget has been climbing progressively and will bring them in line with those of Britain, West Germany and France.

JORDAN

Defense Budget	$ 145,000,000
Population	2,500,000
Manpower in the Armed Forces	69,750
Defense as % of GNP	15%

ARMY

MANPOWER
  65,000 men   (Reserves of 20,000)
GENERAL
  Organized into 2 armored, 2 infantry, 1 mechanized division; plus 1 independent infantry brigade which includes 1 armored car regiment.
PRINCIPAL EQUIPMENT
  <u>Weapons</u>: Light and Heavy Artillery (200 pieces)
           400+ M-47, M-48, M-60 and Centurion Tanks
           290 Armored Cars
           350 Armored Personnel Carriers
  <u>Missiles</u>: TOW

NAVY

MANPOWER
  250 men
GENERAL
  Operates as part of the Army
PRINCIPAL EQUIPMENT
  <u>Ships</u>:   8 Armored Motor Launches

AIR FORCE

MANPOWER
  4,500 men
GENERAL

PRINCIPAL EQUIPMENT

<u>Aircraft</u>:	Fighter-Bombers	30 F-5s
	Interceptors	18 F-104s
		10 F-5s
	Transports	4 C-47s
		2 H.S. Doves
		3 C-119s
		1 C-130B
	Helicopters	6 Alouette IIIs
		3 Whirlwinds
<u>Missiles</u>:	Tigercat	
	TOW	

MISCELLANEOUS DATA

DEFENSE AGREEMENTS
  Arab League Collective Security Pact
MAP TYPE ASSISTANCE RECEIVED FROM
  U.S., U.K., Egypt

JORDAN

INTERNAL SECURITY FORCES
    7,000 Public Security Force, 15,000 Civil Militia
CONSCRIPTION LAW
    Volunteer Forces
MILITARY SCHOOLS
    Royal Military Academy, Royal Staff College; Pilots are trained in the U.S.
NATIONAL FLAG
    Black, white, green (horizontal); a red triangle near the hoist, with a white 7-pointed star on it.
OFFICIAL LANGUAGE
    Arabic
COMBAT EFFECTIVENESS
    Excellent

Defense Budget	$ 32,000,000
Population	13,400,000
Manpower in the Armed Forces	7,650
Defense as % of GNP	3.2%

ARMY

MANPOWER
  6,400 men
GENERAL
  Organized into 4 infantry battalions, 1 parachute company, 1 armored car platoon, support units.
PRINCIPAL EQUIPMENT
  <u>Weapons</u>: Conventional
                 25 Saladin and Ferret Armored Cars
                 Light Artillery

NAVY

MANPOWER
  250 men
PRINCIPAL EQUIPMENT
  <u>Vessels</u>: 4 Patrol Boats

AIR FORCE

MANPOWER
  1,000 men
PRINCIPAL EQUIPMENT

<u>Aircraft</u>:		
	Fighter-Bombers	6 Hunter FGAs
	Counter-Insurgency	12 BAC-167s
	Transports	6 DH Caribous
		10 DH Beavers
	Helicopters	2 Alouette IIs
		2 Bell 47Gs

BASES
  Eastleigh, Embakasi, Nanyuki, Mombasa, Nyeri, Kisumu.

MISCELLANEOUS DATA

DEFENSE AGREEMENTS
  Ethiopia
MAP TYPE ASSISTANCE RECEIVED FROM
  U.K.
INTERNAL SECURITY FORCES
  11,500 men
CONSCRIPTION LAW
  Volunteer forces
NATIONAL FLAG
  Horizontal stripes of black, red, and green, with the center red stripe bordered in white; a shield of black and white markings, and crossed spears behind, appears in the center of the flag.
OFFICIAL LANGUAGE
  English and Swahili
COMBAT EFFECTIVENESS
  Limited

KOREA, NORTH

Defense Budget	$ 800,000,000
Population	15,850,000
Manpower in the Armed Forces	455,000
Defense as % of GNP	N.A.

ARMY

MANPOWER
    400,000 men (Reserves of one-million)
GENERAL
    20 infantry divisions, 2 armored divisions, 3 infantry brigades and 5 armored regiments.
PRINCIPAL EQUIPMENT
    <u>Weapons</u>:   500+ T-54/55 Tanks
                     400 T-34s
                     150 PT-76s
                      50 T-62s
                 5000+ Pieces of Light and Heavy Artillery
                40,000 Trucks

NAVY

MANPOWER
    15,000 men
PRINCIPAL EQUIPMENT
    <u>Vessels</u>:   4 Submarines
                    18 Guided Missile Boats
                    75 Motor Torpedo Boats
                    10 Minesweepers
                    24 Inshore Minesweepers
                    11 Patrol Gunboats
                    26 Ausiliaries
                    70 Armed Junks
    <u>Missiles</u>: Styx

AIR FORCE

MANPOWER
    40,000 men
PRINCIPAL EQUIPMENT
    <u>Aircraft</u>: Bombers   70 IL-28s
                  Fighter-Bombers 30 Su-7s
                                    325 MIG-17s
                                    60 MIG-15s
                  Interceptors   170 MIG-21s
                                    70 MIG-19s
                  Helicopters   30 Mi-4s
                  Transports   100+ AN-2s
BASES
    Ti Taung Kou, Saamchan, Pyong-ni, Namsi, Taechon, Susan, Yenchi, Sinuiju, Yonpo, Wensan, Okean-ni, Pyongyang.

MISCELLANEOUS DATA

DEFENSE AGREEMENTS
    U.S.S.R., Red China
MAP TYPE ASSISTANCE RECEIVED FROM
    U.S.S.R., Red China
INTERNAL SECURITY FORCES
    35,000 men
CONSCRIPTION LAW
    Compulsory service at 18.
NATIONAL FLAG
    A broad center red stripe bordered on top and bottom by a thin white stripe and a broader blue stripe; left of center is a white disc containing a five-pointed red star.
OFFICIAL LANGUAGE
    Korean
COMBAT EFFECTIVENESS
    Excellent
SPECIAL NOTES
    North Korea's relations with the U.S. have continually declined in light of our support of South Korea, and only pressures from the USSR and China have maintained the status quo in the past year.
    Although South Korea seeks an independent course from either, they are almost wholly dependent upon them for wartime resources.

KOREA, SOUTH

Defense Budget	$ 570,000,000
Population	33,095,000
Manpower in the Armed Forces	600,000
Defense as % of GNP	3.5%

ARMY

MANPOWER
  555,000 men
GENERAL
  Organized into 22 infantry divisions, 2 armored divisions, 80 artillery battalions.
PRINCIPAL EQUIPMENT
  <u>Weapons</u>:   1,000+ M-47/48/60 Tanks
            1,000 Armored Vehicles/Personnel Carriers
            2,000 Artillery Pieces - Light and Heavy
  <u>Missiles</u>: Honest John
            Nike Hercules
            Hawk

NAVY

MANPOWER
  17,000 men (Reserves of 35,000)
PRINCIPAL EQUIPMENT
  <u>Vessels</u>:   6 Destroyers
             3 Destroyer Escorts
             4 Frigates
            11 Escort Vessels
             4 Sub Chasers
            11 Coastal Minesweepers
            20 Landing Ships
             2 Motor Torpedo Boats
            20 Landing Ships
             1 Repair Ship
             6 Supply Ships
             4 Oilers
             6 Transports

MARINES

MANPOWER
  20,000 men
GENERAL
  Comprised of one infantry division.

AIR FORCE

MANPOWER
  25,000 men (Reserves of 35,000)

PRINCIPAL EQUIPMENT
   Aircraft: Fighter-Bombers   80 F-5s
                                 30 F-4s
                                 100 F-86Fs
               Reconnaissance   10 RF-5s
               Transports   20 C-46s
                                  6 C-54s
                                  2 Aero Commanders
               Helicopters   6 Sikorsky UH-19s
                                  7 UH-1Ds
                                  2 Bell KH-4s
   Missiles: Sidewinder
               Hawk
               Nike Hercules

BASES
   Pusan, Taegu, P'Ohang, Sachon, Taejon, Pyrontaek, Kusan, Chinhae, Suwon, Kimpo, Seoul, Kangnung, Chungju, Hoensong, Chunchon, Osan -- half are utilized by USAF.

MISCELLANEOUS DATA

DEFENSE AGREEMENTS
   U.S.
MAP TYPE ASSISTANCE RECEIVED FROM
   U.S.
INTERNAL SECURITY FORCES
   2,500,000 Militia
CONSCRIPTION LAW
   Compulsory service at age 20 for 2 1/2 to 3 years; reserve duty until 40.
NATIONAL FLAG
   A divided circle of red (top) and blue (bottom) centered on a white field. A black bar design appears in each corner of the flag.
OFFICIAL LANGUAGE
   Korean
COMBAT EFFECTIVENESS
   Excellent
SPECIAL NOTES
   United States forces in South Korea number just over 42,000.
   Maintenance of this country's armed forces takes 30% of annual federal budget.

KUWAIT

Defense Budget	$ 175,000,000
Population	1,000,000
Manpower in the Armed Forces	10,000
Defense as % of GNP	N.A.

ARMY

MANPOWER
    8,000 men

GENERAL
    Small, well equipped mobile force organized as 3 brigades.

PRINCIPAL EQUIPMENT
    <u>Weapons</u>: Over 100 Vickers and Centurion Tanks
                 Over 300 Armored Cars
                 Limited Artillery

NAVY

MANPOWER
    200 men

GENERAL
    Functions as Coast Guard

PRINCIPAL EQUIPMENT
    <u>Vessels</u>: 16 Patrol Boats
               2 Landing Craft

AIR FORCE

MANPOWER
    1,800 men

PRINCIPAL EQUIPMENT
    <u>Aircraft</u>:

	Fighter-Bombers	12 BAC Lightnings
		4 Hunters
	Armed Trainers	6 Provosts
		12 BAC Strikemasters
		2 BAC Lightning
	Transports	2 D.H. Caribou
		1 Argosy
		1 Devon
		2 Lockheed L-100s
	Interceptors	20 Mirage F1s
	Helicopters	4 Bell 204s
		2 Bell 205s
		1 Westland Whirlwind
		20 Gazelle
		10 Pumas

MISCELLANEOUS DATA

DEFENSE AGREEMENTS
    Arab League Collective Security Pact

MAP TYPE ASSISTANCE RECEIVED FROM
    U.K., U.S.

INTERNAL SECURITY FORCES
    2,500 men
CONSCRIPTION LAW
    Volunteer forces
NATIONAL FLAG
    Green, white and red horizontal stripes joining a
black trapezoid at the staff.
OFFICIAL LANGUAGE
    Arabic
COMBAT EFFECTIVENESS
    Limited

LAOS

Defense Budget	$ 23,000,000
Population	3,415,083
Manpower in the Armed Forces	48,100
Defense as % of GNP	N.A.

DEFENSE ESTABLISHMENT

Since 1954, Laos has been involved in an internal war involving the government and forces of Pathet Lao - the latter in effective control of the Northeastern part of the country. In 1975, Pathet Lao forces moved, broke from the coalition government agreement and took over effective control of the country.

ARMY

MANPOWER
    45,000 men
GENERAL
    Present organization unclear; however, previously organized into infantry battalions.
PRINCIPAL EQUIPMENT
    Weapons: Conventional
                18 PT-76 Tanks
                25 BTR-40 Armored Cars
                 8 M-24 Tanks
                50 Armored Personnel Carriers
                Light and Heavy Artillery

NAVY

MANPOWER
    600 men
PRINCIPAL EQUIPMENT
    Vessels: 20 Patrol Boats
                10 Landing Craft

AIR FORCE

MANPOWER
    2,500 men
PRINCIPAL EQUIPMENT
    Aircraft: Trainers   55 T-28 Armed Trainers
                                 8 C-47 Gunships
                                 5 T-41 Armed Trainers
                Transports   10 C-47s
                                 1 Aero Commander
                                 5 Cessna 185s
                Helicopters   8 Alouette II/IIIs
                                25 UH-34Ds

BASES
    Luang-Prabang, Vientiane, Savannakhet, Pakse

MISCELLANEOUS DATA

DEFENSE AGREEMENTS

MAP TYPE ASSISTANCE RECEIVED FROM
    U.S.S.R., North Vietnamese

INTERNAL SECURITY FORCES
    20,000 men

NATIONAL FLAG
    A three-headed white elephant, standing on 5 steps under a white parasol, against a red field.

OFFICIAL LANGUAGE
    Lao and French

COMBAT EFFECTIVENESS
    Limited

SPECIAL NOTES
    Since defeat of Royal Lao Forces, the country has come under pronounced Soviet and North Vietnamese influence.

LEBANON

Defense Budget $ 112,000,000
Population   2,854,000
Manpower in the Armed Forces   16,250
Defense as % of GNP   6%

DEFENSE ESTABLISHMENT

The Ministry of Defense is in control of the armed forces. They consist primarily of the Army, with integral Navy and Air Forces, supplemented by Security Forces composed of the Gendarmerie and police.

ARMY

MANPOWER
    15,000 men
GENERAL
    Organized primarily for internal security only. Country is too small and lacks resources for any defense against determined foreign aggression.
    Organized into battalion groups; 2 tank, 2 reconnaissance, 9 infantry, 2 artillery, and 1 commando.
PRINCIPAL EQUIPMENT
    <u>Weapons</u>:   Est. over 125 AMX-13, M-41, Charioteer Tanks
                  Est. over 65 Armored Personnel Carriers
                  75 Armored Cars
                  Limited Light Artillery

NAVY

MANPOWER
    250 men
GENERAL
    Coast guard duties.
PRINCIPAL EQUIPMENT
    <u>Vessels</u>:   6 Coastal Patrol Boats
                 6 Small Patrol Boats
                 1 Landing Craft

AIR FORCE

MANPOWER
    1,000 men
GENERAL
    Small and with limited aircraft.
PRINCIPAL EQUIPMENT
    <u>Aircraft</u>: Fighter-Bombers 10 Mirage IIIs
                                      11 Hawker Hunters
                  Helicopters   10 Alouette II/IIIs
                                        6 Bell 212s
                  Transports   1 H.S. Dove
BASES
    Rayak, Khalde, Al Klayat, Latakia, Hama.

MISCELLANEOUS DATA

DEFENSE AGREEMENTS
    Arab League Collective Security Pact
MAP TYPE ASSISTANCE RECEIVED FROM
    U.K., U.S.
INTERNAL SECURITY FORCES
    5,000 men
CONSCRIPTION LAW
    Volunteer forces
NATIONAL FLAG
    Red, white, red (horizontal), with a green cedar on the white stripe.
OFFICIAL LANGUAGE
    Arabic
COMBAT EFFECTIVENESS
    Limited
SPECIAL NOTES

    The Palestine Liberation Organizations' guerrilla groups operate from Lebanon. This has led to growing friction with Israel for whom Lebanon is no match militarily. On December 15, 1974, the Syrian Government vowed defense aid against Israeli attacks if asked for assistance.

    In the fall of 1975, Syrian forces moved into Lebanon to act as stabilizing force to maintain internal peace after a year of serious fighting between conflicting religious groups.

LESOTHO

Defense Budget	$ 1,250,000
Population	1,029,000
Manpower in the Armed Forces	900
Defense as % of GNP	0.09%

Lesotho has no armed forces in the conventional sense.

POLICE (National)

MANPOWER
 900 men

PRINCIPAL EQUIPMENT
 <u>Weapons</u>: Conventional
 Armored Cars

MISCELLANEOUS DATA

DEFENSE AGREEMENTS
 Informal with South Africa
NATIONAL FLAG
 Green and red vertical stripes to the left of a blue field bearing a white conical Basotho hat.
OFFICIAL LANGUAGE
 Sotho
COMBAT EFFECTIVENESS
 Negligible

Defense Budget	$ 4,000,000
Population	1,710,000
Manpower in the Armed Forces	5,200
Defense as % of GNP	1.6%

ARMY

MANPOWER
 5,000 men
GENERAL
 Organized into battalions: 5 infantry, 1 artillery, 1 engineer, plus support units.
PRINCIPAL EQUIPMENT
 Weapons: Conventional
 Armored Cars
 Light Artillery

NAVY

MANPOWER
 200 men
PRINCIPAL EQUIPMENT
 Vessels: 4 Coast Guard Cutters

AIR FORCE

MANPOWER
 25 Men
PRINCIPAL EQUIPMENT
 Aircraft: 2 C-47 Transports
 2 Trainers

MISCELLANEOUS DATA

DEFENSE AGREEMENTS
 U.S.
MAP TYPE ASSISTANCE RECEIVED FROM
 U.S.
INTERNAL SECURITY FORCES
 1,500 men
CONSCRIPTION LAW
 Volunteer forces
NATIONAL FLAG
 Eleven red and white horizontal stripes, with a five-pointed white star on a blue field in the upper left hand corner.
OFFICIAL LANGUAGE
 English
COMBAT EFFECTIVENESS
 Limited

LIBYA

Defense Budget $ 100,000,000
Population   2,409,976
Manpower in the Armed Forces   32,000
Defense as % of GNP   2.5%

ARMY

MANPOWER
    25,000 men
GENERAL
    Organized into 2 armored, 5 infantry brigades; 2 anti-aircraft, 3 artillery battalions.
PRINCIPAL EQUIPMENT
    Weapons: 1,100 Tanks
                    120 Armored Cars
                    800+ Armored Personnel Carriers
                    145 Pieces of Artillery
    Missiles: SS-12
                Vigilant
                Crotale

NAVY

MANPOWER
    2,000 men
PRINCIPAL EQUIPMENT
    Vessels: 1 Frigate
                 2 Coastal Minesweepers
                 8 Patrol Boats
                 1 Corvette
                 3 Coast Guard Vessels
                 2 Inshore Minesweepers
                 1 Repair Ship
    Missiles: Seacat

AIR FORCE

MANPOWER
    5,000 men
PRINCIPAL EQUIPMENT
    Aircraft: Fighter-Bombers/
                 Interceptors   10 F-5s
                                   29 MIG-23s
                                   60 Mirages
               Bombers   12 Tu-22s
               Helicopters   3 Alouette IIIs
                                   12 Mi-8s
                                 4 Bell 47s
               Transports   8 C-130s
                                 7 C-47s
                                 1 Jetstar
    Missiles: SA-6s
                SA-7s
BASES
    Okba Ben Nafi, Benina, El Adem, El Awai, plus strips.

MISCELLANEOUS DATA

DEFENSE AGREEMENTS
    Arab League
MAP TYPE ASSISTANCE RECEIVED FROM
    France, U.K., U.S., U.S.S.R.
INTERNAL SECURITY FORCES
    10,000 men
CONSCRIPTION LAW
    Volunteer forces
NATIONAL FLAG
    A wide horizontal black bank containing a white crescent and star in the center, bordered by a thinner red stripe on top and a thinner green stripe on the bottom.
OFFICIAL LANGUAGE
    Arabic
COMBAT EFFECTIVENESS
    Excellent
SPECIAL NOTES
    Both U.S. and British military bases is Libya have been closed.
    Libya is base for Russian policy in the Arab world and Africa. They funnel Soviet-supplied weapons to guerrilla groups in Africa.
    Libya has offered Malta substantial aid in an attempt to block use of facilities in Malta for ship repair for NATO powers.

LIECHTENSTEIN

Defense Budget	None
Population	21,350
Manpower in the Armed Forces	None
Defense as % of GNP	None

Liechtenstein has no armed forces. They maintain a militia similar to that of Switzerland's.

MISCELLANEOUS DATA

DEFENSE AGREEMENTS
    Foreign affairs handled by Switzerland
INTERNAL SECURITY FORCES
    28 men
NATIONAL FLAG
    Blue and red horizontal stripes, with a golden crown near the staff end of the blue stripes.
OFFICIAL LANGUAGE
    German

Defense Budget	$ 16,000,000
Population	356,818
Manpower in the Armed Forces	550
Defense as % of GNP	0.9%

ARMY

MANPOWER
  550 men
GENERAL
  Organized into 1 infantry battalion of 4 companies
PRINCIPAL EQUIPMENT
  <u>Weapons</u>:   Conventional
               Armored Cars
  <u>Missiles</u>: TOW AT

Luxembourg has neither a Navy or Air Force.

MISCELLANEOUS DATA

DEFENSE AGREEMENTS
  NATO
INTERNAL SECURITY FORCES
  350 men
CONSCRIPTION LAW
  Volunteer Forces
NATIONAL FLAG
  Tri-color of red, white and blue horizontal stripes.
OFFICIAL LANGUAGE
  French and German

MALAGASY REPUBLIC
(MADAGASCAR)

Defense Budget	$ 18,000,000
Population	7,254,000
Manpower in the Armed Forces	4,500
Defense as % of GNP	1.7%

ARMY

MANPOWER
  4,000 men

GENERAL
  Organized into 4 infantry and 1 parachute company, 1 reconnaissance squadron, 1 artillery battery, and 1 engineer battalion.

PRINCIPAL EQUIPMENT
  Weapons: Conventional
             Ferret Armored Cars
             Light Artillery
             4 M-3 Tanks

NAVY

MANPOWER
  300 men (includes 1 Marine Company)

PRINCIPAL EQUIPMENT
  Vessels: 2 Patrol Vessels
             1 Tender
             1 Training Ship

AIR FORCE

MANPOWER
  400 men

PRINCIPAL EQUIPMENT
  Aircraft: Transports   3 C-47s
                             10 Broussards
                             5 MD-312s
              Fighters   12 A-1Ds
              Helicopters   2 Alouette II/IIIs

BASES
  Diego-Surarez, Ivato, Arivoniamamo, Fort Dauphin, Tamatave, Majunga, Tulear.

MISCELLANEOUS DATA

DEFENSE AGREEMENTS
  France

MAP TYPE ASSISTANCE RECEIVED FROM
  France, West Germany, Israel

INTERNAL SECURITY FORCES
  5,900 men

CONSCRIPTION LAW
  2 years' compulsory service; civil service alternative.

NATIONAL FLAG
  A white vertical stripe at the staff and 2 horizontal stripes, the upper red, the lower green.

OFFICIAL LANGUAGE
    Malagasy and French
COMBAT EFFECTIVENESS
    Limited
SPECIAL NOTES
    France has about 2,000 troops stationed in Country.

MALAWI

Defense Budget $ 3,000,000
Population 5,040,000
Manpower in the Armed Forces 2,000
Defense as % of GNP 1.0%

ARMY

MANPOWER
    2,000 men
GENERAL
    Comprises 2 infantry battalions, and 1 armored car squadron.
PRINCIPAL EQUIPMENT
    Weapons: Conventional
                10 Scout Cars

NAVY

None.

AIR FORCE

MANPOWER
    25 men
PRINCIPAL EQUIPMENT
    Aircraft: 2 Islander Transports
                2 HS-748s Transports

MISCELLANEOUS DATA

DEFENSE AGREEMENTS
    None.
MAP TYPE ASSISTANCE RECEIVED FROM
    U.K.
INTERNAL SECURITY FORCES
    5,900 men
CONSCRIPTION LAW
    Volunteer forces
NATIONAL FLAG
    Three horizontal stripes of black, red and green, with a red rising sun on the black stripe.
OFFICIAL LANGUAGE
    English
COMBAT EFFECTIVENESS
    Limited
SPECIAL NOTES
    There is only one service, the Army in Malawi.

Defense Budget	$ 254,000,000
Population	11,930,000
Manpower in the Armed Forces	65,000
Defense as % of GNP	4.8%

ARMY

MANPOWER
    55,000 men (Reserves of 25,000)
GENERAL
    Organized into 25 infantry battalions, 2 reconnaissance regiments, 3 artillery regiments, 3 communications regiments, and one special unit.
PRINCIPAL EQUIPMENT
    <u>Weapons:</u>   600+ Ferret Armored Cars
                   100+ Armored Personnel Carriers
                    60 105mm Howitzers
                    Light Artillery

NAVY

MANPOWER
    4,000 men
PRINCIPAL EQUIPMENT
    <u>Vessels:</u>   2 Destroyer Escorts
                  1 ASW Frigate with Seacat Missiles
                  6 Coastal Minesweepers
                24 Patrol Craft
                  4 Fast Patrol Boats
                  1 Training Tender
                  1 Survey Vessel
                  1 Repair Boat
                  4 Motor Torpedo Boats
                20 Landing Craft
    <u>Missiles:</u> Exocet
                  SS-11
                  SS-12

AIR FORCE

MANPOWER
    5,000 men
PRINCIPAL EQUIPMENT
    <u>Aircraft:</u> Fighter-Bombers   16 CA-27 Sabre
                                     14 F-5s
                                     16 SF-260s
                    Counter/
                      Insurgency   20 CL-41G Tebuans
                    Transports   8 Herald 401s
                                     30 DH Caribous
                                      5 HS Doves
                                      3 HS Herons
                                      2 HS 125
                                      6 C-130s
                                      2 F-28s

MALAYSIA   141

                    Helicopters   25 Alouette IIIs
                                        6 Bell 47s
                                        5 Bell 206s
                                       15 Sikorsky S-61s
BASES
    Kuala Lumpur, Kuantan, Alor Star, Butterworth, Labuan,
Kuching, East Malaysia.

MISCELLANEOUS DATA

DEFENSE AGREEMENTS
    Anglo-Malaysian Mutual Defense Treaty
MAP TYPE ASSISTANCE RECEIVED FROM
    U.S., U.K.
INTERNAL SECURITY FORCES
    10,000 men
CONSCRIPTION LAW
    Volunteer forces
NATIONAL FLAG
    Red and white stripes with blue field in upper left
corner containing crescent and star in yellow.
OFFICIAL LANGUAGE
    Malay
COMBAT EFFECTIVENESS
    Excellent
SPECIAL NOTES
    Malaysia has been experiencing substantial increases
in Communist guerrilla activity over past year and plans
joint action with Thailand to quell this problem affecting both states.

MALI

Defense Budget	$ 10,000,000
Population	5,700,000
Manpower in the Armed Forces	4,000
Defense as % of GNP	2.8%

ARMY

MANPOWER
   3,400 men

GENERAL
   Organized into 3 infantry battalions, 1 armored unit, and 1 paratroop company; plus support units.

PRINCIPAL EQUIPMENT
   Weapons: Conventional
              10 T-34 Tanks
              Armored Personnel Carriers
              Light Artillery

NAVY

None.
Army also operates small river patrol force equipped with three patrol boats and 40 men.

AIR FORCE

MANPOWER
   400 men

PRINCIPAL EQUIPMENT
   Aircraft: 2 MIG-15s
               6 MIG-17s
               2 C-47 Transports
               2 Broussards
               2 Mi-4 Helicopters

BASES
   Bamako and Gao.

MISCELLANEOUS DATA

MAP TYPE ASSISTANCE RECEIVED FROM
   France, U.S., U.S.S.R., Red China

INTERNAL SECURITY FORCES
   1,200 men

CONSCRIPTION LAW
   Compulsory service for 2 years.

NATIONAL FLAG
   Three vertical stripes of green, yellow and red.

OFFICIAL LANGUAGE
   French

COMBAT EFFECTIVENESS
   Limited

MAURITANIA

Defense Budget $ 10,000,000
Population 1,300,000
Manpower in the Armed Forces 1,700
Defense as % of GNP 3.5%

DEFENSE ESTABLISHMENT

There is a Minister of Defense directly responsible to the President. Army, Navy and Air Force geared to internal control rather than external defense. Military heavily involved in civic action projects.

ARMY

MANPOWER
 1,500 men
GENERAL
 1 infantry battalion; 3 recon squadrons, 1 para-commando company.
PRINCIPAL EQUIPMENT
 Weapons: Light Only
  15 Armored Cars

NAVY

MANPOWER
 50 men
GENERAL
 Coast Guard role
PRINCIPAL EQUIPMENT
 Vessels: 4 Patrol Boats

AIR FORCE

MANPOWER
 150 men
GENERAL
 Transport and Communications role only.
PRINCIPAL EQUIPMENT
 Aircraft: Transports 4 C-47s
   4 MH Broussards
  Liaison 2 Aeromacchi AL-60s
BASES
 Nouakcott, Nouadhibou, Atar, F'Derik, Bir Moghrein, Akjoujt, Kaedi, Rosso, Kiffa, Ayoun-el-Atrous.

MISCELLANEOUS DATA

DEFENSE AGREEMENTS
 Union Africaine et Malgache
MAP TYPE ASSISTANCE RECEIVED FROM
 France

INTERNAL SECURITY FORCES
    Gendarmerie - 300
    Civil Police - 1000
NATIONAL FLAG
    Four horizontal stripes of red, blue, yellow and
green.
OFFICIAL LANGUAGE
    English
CONSCRIPTION LAW
    Volunteer forces
COMBAT EFFECTIVENESS
    Extremely limited

MEXICO

Defense Budget	$ 344,000,000
Population	60,150,000
Manpower in the Armed Forces	70,000
Defense as % of GNP	0.9%

ARMY

MANPOWER
    55,000 men

GENERAL
    Organized as: 50 infantry, 2 artillery battalions, 20 cavalty regiments, 1 mechanized cavalry regiment, AA, eginner and support units.

PRINCIPAL EQUIPMENT
    Weapons: 35 M-4 Tanks
                    75 Armored Personnel Carriers
                    300 Armored Cars
                    Light and Heavy Artillery

NAVY

MANPOWER
    9,000 men (plus 2,000 Marines)

PRINCIPAL EQUIPMENT
    Vessels: 8 Frigates
                  2 Destroyers
                30 Patrol Boats
                18 Escort Vessels
                4 Minesweepers
                6 Sub Chasers
                6 Landing Craft
                4 Transports
                1 Presidential Yacht
    Aircraft: 5 PBY-2s
                  5 Bell 47s
                  4 Alouette IIIs
                  3 N.B. Islanders
                  2 C-45s
                  4 Cessna 180s

AIR FORCE

MANPOWER
    6,000 men

PRINCIPAL EQUIPMENT
    Aircraft: Fighter-Bombers   12 Vampires
                  Counter-
                      Insurgency   15 T-33s
                                      25 T-28s
                Reconnaissance   15 AT-11s

Transports	6 C-47s
	5 C-54s
	2 C-118s
	1 DC-7
	5 Aravas
	1 MU-25
	3 Islanders
	1 Jetstar
Helicopters	14 Bell 47s
	10 Bell 205s
	1 Bell UH-1N
	1 Hiller UH-12
	2 Bell 206s
	7 Alouette IIs
	9 Alouette IIIs

BASES
    Santa Lucia, Ciudad Ixtepee, Ensenada, Cozumel, Zapoan, Puebla, Acapulco, Merida.

MISCELLANEOUS DATA

DEFENSE AGREEMENTS
    Rio Pact
MAP TYPE ASSISTANCE RECEIVED FROM
    U.S.
INTERNAL SECURITY FORCES
    60,000 men
CONSCRIPTION LAW
    Primarily volunteer forces. However, males age 18 serve one year of weekly drills similar to U.S. National Guardsmen.
NATIONAL FLAG
    Green, red and white vertical stripes with the national coat of arms in center.
OFFICIAL LANGUAGE
    Spanish
COMBAT EFFECTIVENESS

SPECIAL NOTES
    Over the past years, Mexico has had a significant guerrilla insurgency problem. However, due to the death of Lucio Cabanas, the guerrilla leader they now estimate that fewer than 100 members of his forces are active.

MONGOLIA

Defense Budget	$ 55,000,000
Population	1,462,876
Manpower in the Armed Forces	29,000
Defense as % of GNP	6.5%

ARMY

MANPOWER
28,000 men (Reserves of 30,000)

GENERAL
Organized into 2 infantry divisions and supporting units.

PRINCIPAL EQUIPMENT
- Weapons: 150+ T-34/T-54/T-55 Tanks
  100 Armored Personnel Carriers
  Light and Heavy Artillery
- Missiles: Snapper AT

NAVY

None.

AIR FORCE

MANPOWER
1000 men

GENERAL
Operates as part of Army.

PRINCIPAL EQUIPMENT
- Aircraft:
  - Fighter-Bombers: 10 MIG-15s
  - Helicopters: 10 Mi-1/Mi-4s
  - Transports: 30 An-2, Il-14, An-24s
  - Trainers: Yak-11, Yak-18, MIG-15UTI
- Missiles: 2 SAM Battalions with Guidelines

MISCELLANEOUS DATA

DEFENSE AGREEMENTS
COMECON

MAP TYPE ASSISTANCE RECEIVED FROM
U.S.S.R.

INTERNAL SECURITY FORCES
17,500 men

CONSCRIPTION LAW
2 years' compulsory service for all males.

NATIONAL FLAG
Vertical stripes of red, blue and red with a yellow star and traditional symbols on the left.

OFFICIAL LANGUAGE
Khalkha Mongolian

COMBAT EFFECTIVENESS
Limited

Defense Budget	$ 190,000,000
Population	16,000,000
Manpower in the Armed Forces	61,000
Defense as % of GNP	3.5%

DEFENSE ESTABLISHMENT

The King is supreme commander and chief of staff. Operational and administrative control is via the Ministry of Defense.

The Royal Armed Forces of Morocco consist of the Army, Navy and Air Force. The Gendarmerie are operationally subordinate to the Army.

The armed forces have the dual mission of providing the external defense and maintenance of internal control. The Army is engaged in extensive civic action programs.

ARMY

MANPOWER
    55,000 men

GENERAL
    The country is divided into three military zones and one independent sector.
    Organized into three motorized brigades, 3 armored battalions, 16 infantry battalions, 5 camel corps battalions, 3 desert cavalry battalions, engineer battalion and Royal Guards battalion.

PRINCIPAL EQUIPMENT
    Weapons: 250 T-54 and AMX-13 Tanks
                    110 Armored Personnel Carriers
                    85 Armored Cars
                    Light and Heavy Artillery (est. 300 pcs.)

NAVY

MANPOWER
    2,000 men

GENERAL
    The Navy is subordinate to the army general staff, and has its headquarters and main operating base at Casablanca. (Has 500 man marine unit included in above manpower).

PRINCIPAL EQUIPMENT
    Vessels: 1 Frigate
                  4 Patrol Boats
                  2 Corvettes
                  1 Landing Craft

AIR FORCE

MANPOWER
    4,000 men

PRINCIPAL EQUIPMENT

Aircraft:
	Fighter-Bombers	12 MIG-17s
	Interceptors	24 F-5s
	Transports	6 C-130s
		10 C-47s
		11 C-119s
	Helicopters	24 Bell 204s
		7 Alouette IIIs
		4 HH-43Bs

BASES
Ben Guerir, Rabat-Sale, Meknes, Marrakech, Mellilla, Sidi Slimane, Port Lyautey, Fez, Boulhat, Nouasseur, Casablance, Kenitra.

MISCELLANEOUS DATA

DEFENSE AGREEMENTS
    Arab League Collective Security Pact
MAP TYPE ASSISTANCE RECEIVED FROM
    France, Spain, U.S., U.S.S.R.
INTERNAL SECURITY FORCES
    24,300 men
CONSCRIPTION LAW
    18 months' service for all males at 18.
MILITARY SCHOOLS
    Royal Military Academy
NATIONAL FLAG
    Red, with a green 5-pointed star in the center.
OFFICIAL LANGUAGE
    Arabic
COMBAT EFFECTIVENESS
    Excellent

NEPAL

Defense Budget	$ 8,500,000
Population	11,556,000
Manpower in the Armed Forces	20,500
Defense as % of GNP	N.A.

DEFENSE ESTABLISHMENT

The Army is the only defense force with a small aviation contingent. No formal defense structure exists with King as commander-in-chief of the armed forces.

ARMY

MANPOWER
    20,000 men
GENERAL
    Organized into 5 infantry brigades, 1 parachute battalion, and 1 artillery regiment.
PRINCIPAL EQUIPMENT
    Weapons: Light Artillery
                Armored Cars

NAVY

None.

AIR FORCE

MANPOWER
    500 men
GENERAL
    Functions under control of Army.
PRINCIPAL EQUIPMENT
    Aircraft: Transports   2 Skyvans
                                2 C-47s
                Helicopters   1 Alouette III
BASES
    Katmandu and regional airstrips.

MISCELLANEOUS DATA

DEFENSE AGREEMENTS
    India
MAP TYPE ASSISTANCE RECEIVED FROM
    U.K.
INTERNAL SECURITY FORCES
    10,000 men
CONSCRIPTION LAW
    Volunteer force
NATIONAL FLAG
    Two red right-angle triangles bordered in blue at the hoist; the upper with a white moon crescent, the lower with a white sun.
OFFICIAL LANGUAGE
    Nepalese
COMBAT EFFECTIVENESS
    Extremely limited.

NETHERLANDS

    Defense Budget $ 1,967,000,000
    Population   13,733,000
    Manpower in the Armed Forces   114,000
    Defense as % of GNP   3.8%

ARMY

MANPOWER
    75,000 men (Reserves of 350,000)
GENERAL
    Organized into 4 mechanized infantry and 2 armored brigades, 2 missile battalions.
PRINCIPAL EQUIPMENT
    Weapons: 400 Centurion Tanks
                500 Leopard Tanks
                140 AMX-13 Tanks
                1400 Armored Personnel Carriers
                Light and Heavy Artillery
    Missiles: TOW AT
                Honest John
                Nord SS-12

NAVY

MANPOWER
    19,000 men (Reserves of 70,000)
PRINCIPAL EQUIPMENT
    Vessels: 2 Cruisers (Terrier Missiles)
                6 Submarines
                12 Destroyers
                6 Frigates (Seacat Missiles)
                6 Corvettes
                25 Coastal Minesweepers
                16 Inshore Minesweepers
                5 Patrol Vessels
                3 Survey Ships
                1 Fast Combat Support Ship
                7 Landing Craft
                1 Boom Defense Vessel
                2 Torpedo Tenders
                3 Supply Ships
                5 Diving Vessels
                2 Training Ships
                40 Auxiliaries
    Aircraft: 15 SP-2 Neptunes ASW Patrol
                8 P-13 Atlantique ASW Patrol
                7 Bell UH-1 Helicopters
                12 Westland Wasps

AIR FORCE

MANPOWER
    20,000 men (Reserves of 70,000)

PRINCIPAL EQUIPMENT
<u>Aircraft</u>: Fighter-Bombers 75 NF-5As
                                 45 F-104s
                 Interceptors   45 F-104s
                 Reconnaissance 20 RF-104s
                 Transports   12 F-27s
                 Helicopters   75 Alouette IIIs
                 Liaison   9 DH Beavers
                                 60 Piper L-18s
<u>Missiles</u>: Sidewinder
            Nike Hercules
            Hawk

BASES
    Eindhoven, Volkel, Soesterburg, Twente, Leeuwarden, Deelen, Gilze-Rijen.

MISCELLANEOUS DATA

DEFENSE AGREEMENTS
    NATO
MAP TYPE ASSISTANCE RECEIVED FROM
    U.S.
INTERNAL SECURITY FORCES
    7,800 men
CONSCRIPTION LAW
    Compulsory service for all males; 16-18 monthsiin Army, 21-24 months in Navy, and 18-21 months in Air Force.
NATIONAL FLAG
    Red, white and blue horizontal stripes.
OFFICIAL LANGUAGE
    Dutch
COMBAT EFFECTIVENESS
    Excellent
SPECIAL NOTES
    The Netherlands also has responsibility for defense of overseas territories in the West Indies.

NEW ZEALAND

Defense Budget	$ 225,000,000
Population	3,148,000
Manpower in the Armed Forces	13,085
Defense as % of GNP	3.7%

ARMY

MANPOWER
 5,600 men (Reserves of 11,700)

GENERAL
 Organized into 1 combat brigade group, 1 regular and 6 territorial battalions.

PRINCIPAL EQUIPMENT
 Weapons:
  10 M-41 Tanks
  4 Centurions
  9 Ferret Armored Cars
  60 Armored Personnel Carriers
  Light and Limited Heavy Artillery

NAVY

MANPOWER
 3,000 men (Reserves of 1,000)

PRINCIPAL EQUIPMENT
 Vessels:
  4 Escorts with Seacat Missiles
  2 Escort Minesweepers
  1 Survey Vessel
  1 Patrol Vessel
  12 Seaward Patrol Vessels
  1 Antarctica Support Ship
  2 Tenders
  4 Auxiliaries
 Missiles: Seacat
 Aircraft:
  2 Westland Wasps
  5 T-55 Vampire Support Aircraft

AIR FORCE

MANPOWER
 4,485 men (Reserves of 8,000)

PRINCIPAL EQUIPMENT

Aircraft:		
Fighter-Bombers	10	A-4s
	16	BAC-167s
	4	TA-4Ks
Reconnaissance	5	P-3 Orions
Transports	5	C-130s
	9	Bristol 170s
	16	HS Devons
	6	C-47s
Helicopters	13	Bell UH-1Ds
	12	Bell OH-13s

MISCELLANEOUS DATA

DEFENSE AGREEMENTS
   U.K., Australia, U.S., ANZUS
MAP TYPE ASSISTANCE RECEIVED FROM
   U.S.
INTERNAL SECURITY FORCES
   900 men
CONSCRIPTION LAW
   All male citizens 18 to 21 serve short period, followed by 3 years' part-time service.
NATIONAL FLAG
   A blue field, with the British Union Jack in the upper left hand the Southern Cross in white on the right.
OFFICIAL LANGUAGE
   English
COMBAT EFFECTIVENESS
   Limited
SPECIAL NOTES
   New Zealand joined with Australia to oppose a British-American agreement for the U.S. to build-up naval facilities at Diego Garcia in the Indian Ocean.

NICARAGUA

Defense Budget	$ 15,000,000
Population	2,160,000
Manpower in the Armed Forces	7,110
Defense as % of GNP	2.0%

ARMY

MANPOWER
   5,410 men (Reserves of 4,000)
GENERAL
   Organized into 15 infantry companys, 1 motorized detachment, engineers, and 1 AA battery.
PRINCIPAL EQUIPMENT
   Weapons: Conventional
              10 Light Tanks
              40 Armored Cars
              10 Armored Personnel Carriers

NAVY

MANPOWER
   200 men
GENERAL
   Coast Guard duties only.
PRINCIPAL EQUIPMENT
   Vessels: 6 Patrol Boats
              1 Training Vessel

AIR FORCE

MANPOWER
   1,500 men
PRINCIPAL EQUIPMENT
   Aircraft: Bombers   6 B-26s
              Counter-
                Insurgency   4 T-33s
              Transports   3 C-47s
                                  10 Cessna 180s
                                   1 Arava
BASES
   Managua and Puerto Cabeza

MISCELLANEOUS DATA

DEFENSE AGREEMENTS
   Rio Pact
MAP TYPE ASSISTANCE RECEIVED FROM
   U.S.
INTERNAL SECURITY FORCES
   4,000 men
CONSCRIPTION LAW
   Selective service for 3 years.

NATIONAL FLAG
    Horizontal stripes of blue, white, blue with national coat of arms in the center.
OFFICIAL LANGUAGE
    Spanish
COMBAT EFFECTIVENESS
    Limited
SPECIAL NOTES
    Country has been under dictatorial type military control since 1936.
    Guerrilla activity is continual with somewhere close to 100 Nicaraguan soldiers slain in the past year.

NIGER

Defense Budget	$ 6,000,000
Population	4,668,000
Manpower in the Armed Forces	2,100
Defense as % of GNP	2.5%

ARMY

MANPOWER
   2,000 men

GENERAL
   Comprises five infantry battalions, 4 parachute and commando companys, engineer and reconnaissance units.

PRINCIPAL EQUIPMENT
   Weapons: Conventional
              Armored Cars
              Light Artillery

NAVY

None.

Army responsible for river patrol utilizing about 200 men and equipped with 3 motor gunboats, 1 patrol vessel and several landing craft.

AIR FORCE

MANPOWER
   100 men

PRINCIPAL EQUIPMENT
   Aircraft: 1 C-47 Transport
               4 Noratlas Transports
               4 Broussard Liaison

BASES
Niamey, Zinder, Agadez, Tahous, Maradi.

MISCELLANEOUS DATA

DEFENSE AGREEMENTS
   France, Ivory Coast, Union Africane et Malgache

MAP TYPE ASSISTANCE RECEIVED FROM
   U.S., France

INTERNAL SECURITY FORCES
   1,700 men

CONSCRIPTION LAW
   2 years' compulsory service.

NATIONAL FLAG
   Horizontal stripes of orange, white and green with an orange disc in the center.

OFFICIAL LANGUAGE
   French

COMBAT EFFECTIVENESS
   Limited

SPECIAL NOTES
   Military coup took over country in April 1974; a second group attempted to oust the present government in August of 1975, but failed.

NIGERIA

```
Defense Budget                    $ 648,000,000
Population                          79,758,000
Manpower in the Armed Forces           250,000
Defense as % of GNP                       8.1%
```

ARMY

MANPOWER
 240,000 men (Reserves of 100,000+)
GENERAL
 Organized into 5 infantry divisions, 3 armored reconnaissance regiments, 3 artillery and 3 engineer regiments.
PRINCIPAL EQUIPMENT
 Weapons: 200 Saladin Armored Cars
             35 AML-60/90s
             10 Ferret Scout Cars
             25 Saracen Armored Personnel Carriers
             10 Fox Scout Cars
              5 Scorpion Tanks
            Light Artillery

NAVY

MANPOWER
 1,700 men (Reserves of 2,000)
PRINCIPAL EQUIPMENT
 Vessels: 1 ASW Frigate
             6 Seaward Defense Boats
             2 Minesweeping Launches
             2 Corvettes
             1 Landing Craft
             1 Dispatch Vessel
             2 Survey Vessels

AIR FORCE

MANPOWER
 5,000 men (Reserves of 4,000)
PRINCIPAL EQUIPMENT
 Aircraft: Bombers   6 Il-28s
            Fighter-Bombers   6 MIG-21s
                                 12 MIG-17s
                                  5 MIG-15s
            Counter-
              Insurgency   15 Delfins
            Transports   3 C-130s
                                  6 C-47s
                                  6 F-27s
            Helicopters   3 Whirlwinds
                                  5 Alouette IIs

NIGERIA

MISCELLANEOUS DATA

DEFENSE AGREEMENTS
    U.K., OAU
MAP TYPE ASSISTANCE RECEIVED FROM
    Canada, India, Pakistan, U.K., U.S., U.S.S.R., West Germany, Netherlands, Czechoslovakia.
INTERNAL SECURITY FORCES
    24,000 men
CONSCRIPTION LAW
    Volunteer forces
NATIONAL FLAG
    Vertical stripes of green, white, green.
OFFICIAL LANGUAGE
    English
COMBAT EFFECTIVENESS
    Limited
SPECIAL NOTES
    Military coup took over government in July of 1969.
    Soviet anticipates establishing air and naval bases in Nigeria and construction personnel are in initial stages today.

Defense Budget	$ 690,000,000
Population	4,017,000
Manpower in the Armed Forces	35,000
Defense as % of GNP	3.6%

ARMY

MANPOWER
   18,000 men (Reserves of 160,000)

GENERAL
   Organized into 5 regional commands, 5 regimental combat teams, 4 tank companys.

PRINCIPAL EQUIPMENT
   Weapons: 80 Leopard Tanks
              40 M-48 Tanks
              47 M-24 Tanks
                 M-8 Armored Cars
                 M-113 Armored Personnel Carriers
                 BV-202 Armored Personnel Carriers
                 Light and Heavy Artillery
   Missiles: TOW AT

NAVY

MANPOWER
   8,500 men (Reserves of 18,000)

PRINCIPAL EQUIPMENT
   Vessels: 15 Submarines
               5 Destroyer Escorts
               5 Coastal Minelayers
              10 Coastal Minesweepers
              26 Motor Torpedo Boats
              20 Fast Gunboats with Penguin Missiles
               1 Training Ship
               2 Depot Ships
               1 Royal Yacht
               5 Coast Guard Vessels
               7 Landing Craft
   Missiles: Penguin

AIR FORCE

MANPOWER
   9,000 men (Reserves of 19,000)

PRINCIPAL EQUIPMENT
   Aircraft: Fighter-Bombers   48 F-5s
               Interceptors   20 F-104s
               Reconnaissance   16 RF-5As
               ASW Patrol   5 P-3 Orions
               Transports   6 C-130s
                                   4 DH Otters
                                  20 Falcons
               Helicopters   30 Bell UH-1Bs
                                  10 Sea Kings

NORWAY

    <u>Missiles</u>:   Nike Hercules
                    Bullpup
                    Sidewinder

BASES
    Gardermoen, Sola, Rygge, Vaernes, Bodo, Orlandet, Bardufoss, Andoya, Banak.

MISCELLANEOUS DATA

DEFENSE AGREEMENTS
    NATO
MAP TYPE ASSISTANCE RECEIVED FROM
    U.S.
INTERNAL SECURITY FORCES
    70,000 men
CONSCRIPTION LAW
    Compulsory service at age 20 for 12-15 months in Army or 18 months in Navy or Air Force.
NATIONAL FLAG
    An extended white bordered blue cross on a red field.
OFFICIAL LANGUAGE
    Norwegian
COMBAT EFFECTIVENESS
    Excellent
SPECIAL NOTES
    Norway faces a difficult diplomatic issue with the U.S.S.R. over 60,000 square miles of the Barents Sea known to contain vast oil reserves.

Defense Budget $ 500,000,000
Population   750,000
Manpower in the Armed Forces   14,200
Defense as % of GNP   N.A.

ARMY

MANPOWER
   12,000 men
GENERAL
   Organized into battalions: 4 infantry, 1 armored cavalry, 1 frontier guards, and artillery and communications units.
PRINCIPAL EQUIPMENT
   Weapons: 100 Armored Cars
               Light Artillery Only
   Missiles: Rapier

NAVY

MANPOWER
   200 men
PRINCIPAL EQUIPMENT
   Vessels: 3 Patrol Boats
               3 Armored Chows
               1 Yacht

AIR FORCE

MANPOWER
   2,000 men
GENERAL
   Newly formed small force with three key bases.
PRINCIPAL EQUIPMENT
   Aircraft: Armed Trainers   20 BAC 167s
               Transports   5 Viscounts
                                  2 D.H. Caribous
                                 16 Short Skyvans
                                  4 D.H. Beavers
               Helicopters   17 Bell 205s
                                  4 Bell 206s
                                  5 Bell 205As
                                  6 Bell 214s

MISCELLANEOUS DATA

DEFENSE AGREEMENTS
   U.K., Saudi Arabia, Iran
MAP TYPE ASSISTANCE RECEIVED FROM
   Saudi Arabia, Iran
INTERNAL SECURITY FORCES
   4,000 men

OMAN

CONSCRIPTION LAW
   Volunteer forces
NATIONAL FLAG
   Red, white and green with crossed swords in red sector.
OFFICIAL LANGUAGE
   Arabic
COMBAT EFFECTIVENESS
   Limited
SPECIAL NOTES

The U.S. has asked Britain for the use of airfield facilities on Masira Island, off the east coast of Oman to counter growing Soviet air power in the area.

Iran has "guaranteed" to assist Oman in safeguarding its airspace against foreign intruders. This move apparently a warning to the radical government of Southern Yemen, which has sent aircraft over Oman in recent years.

More than 1,000 Iranian infantry troops are serving in Oman.

PAKISTAN

Defense Budget $ 573,000,000
Population   42,978,261
Manpower in the Armed Forces   390,000
Defense as % of GNP   6.0%

DEFENSE ESTABLISHMENT

The President is the Supreme Commander of the Defense Services. Under present conditions, the Commander in Chief of each service is responsible directly to him, officiating as the Minister of Defense.

ARMY

MANPOWER
    365,000 men (Reserves of 500,000)
GENERAL
    Organized into 2 armored, 13 infantry divisions, 2 independent armored, 1 air defense brigade. Three squadrons of aircraft operate with Army.
PRINCIPAL EQUIPMENT
    Weapons: Est. 1,200 medium Tanks - (M-47/48, T-55/59s)
                 Est. 500 Armored Personnel Carriers
                       225 Light Tanks - M-24/41, PT-76s
                 Est. 1,000 Pieces of Artillery
    Missiles: TOW
                 Cobra
    Aircraft: Liaison   50 Cessna O-1s
                 Helicopters   20 Alouette IIIs
                                     12 Bell 47Gs
                                     12 Mi-8s

NAVY

MANPOWER
    10,000 men (Reserves of 5,000)
PRINCIPAL EQUIPMENT
    Vessels: 3 Submarines
                 1 Light Cruiser (Training)
                 4 Destroyers
                 4 Frigates
                 7 Coastal Minesweepers
                 9 Patrol Boats
                 2 Oilers
                 1 Water Carrier
    Aircraft: Helicopters   2 UH-19s
                                     6 Sea Kings

AIR FORCE

MANPOWER
    15,000 men (Reserves of 8,000)

PAKISTAN 165

GENERAL
    Organized with operational units in fighter, bomber and transport wings.

PRINCIPAL EQUIPMENT
    Aircraft:

	Fighter-Bombers	28 Mirage Vs
		130 MIG-19s
		50 F-86s
		70 CF-86s
	Interceptors	21 Mirage IIIs
	Transports	7 C-130s
		1 F-27
		1 Aero Commander
	Reconnaissance	4 RT-33s
		2 RB-57s
		3 Mirage IIIs
	Helicopters	6 Sea Kings ASW
		4 Alouette IIIs
		2 UH-19s
		4 HH-43s

    Missiles: Sidewinder
               Matra

BASES
    Mauripur, Peshawar, Chaklala, Risalpur, Sargodha, Samungli, Drigh Road, Kohat, Musroor, Murid, Chaderi, Risalawala, Mianwali, Multan, Shorkot.

MISCELLANEOUS DATA

DEFENSE AGREEMENTS
    CENTO

MAP TYPE ASSISTANCE RECEIVED FROM
    Red China, U.S.

INTERNAL SECURITY FORCES
    National Guard - 10,000; Civil Armed Forces - 40,000

CONSCRIPTION LAW
    Selective service - 2 years

MILITARY SCHOOLS
    Command and Staff College, Army Aviation School, Pakistan Military Academy, Pakistan Naval Academy, Air Force College, Air Force Staff College, Air Force College of Aeronautical Engineering, School of Military Engineering, School of Infantry and Tactics, School of Electric and Mechanical Engineers, School of Artillery, Armored Corps School, School of Signal Communications.

NATIONAL FLAG
    Green, with a white vertical stripe at the hoist and a white crescent and a five-pointed star in the center.

OFFICIAL LANGUAGE
    Urdu and Bengali

COMBAT EFFECTIVENESS
    Excellent

SPECIAL NOTES

Submarine Ghazi sunk in India-Pakistan war on December 4, 1971.

Destroyer Khaibar and 3 patrol craft also sunk in December, 1971.

The U.S. has been offered the right to construct an airbase and naval base on the shore of the Arabian Sea close to the Iranian frontier.

Pakistan has withdrawn from SEATO Pact.

PARAGUAY

```
Defense Budget              $ 21,000,000
Population                    3,633,000
Manpower in the Armed Forces     20,500
Defense as % of GNP                 4.0%
```

ARMY

MANPOWER
    17,500 men (Reserves of 60,000)

GENERAL
    Organized into 1 cavalry, 3 infantry brigades, 5 engineer battalions, and 3 artillery batteries.

PRINCIPAL EQUIPMENT
    <u>Weapons:</u> Conventional
                  10 M-4 Tanks
                  Armored Personnel Carriers
                  Light Artillery
    <u>Aircraft:</u> 6 Piper Liaison
                  3 Bell OH-13s

NAVY

MANPOWER
    2,000 men

PRINCIPAL EQUIPMENT
    <u>Vessels:</u> 5 Armored River Gunboats
                 3 Patrol Boats
                 6 Picket Vessels
                 1 Training Ship
                 2 Landing Craft (1 with helicopters)

AIR FORCE

MANPOWER
    1,000 men

PRINCIPAL EQUIPMENT
    <u>Aircraft:</u> Counter-
                    Insurgency   6 T-6s
                Transports   10 C-47s
                                   2 C-54s
                                   3 C-45s
                                   1 DH Dove
                Helicopters   20 Bell 47s
                                   3 Hiller UH-12s
                Trainers   14 T-6s
                                  20 Uirapurus

BASES
    Asuncion

MISCELLANEOUS DATA

DEFENSE AGREEMENTS
    Rio Pact

MAP TYPE ASSISTANCE RECEIVED FROM
 U.S.
INTERNAL SECURITY FORCES
 8,500 men
CONSCRIPTION LAW
 2 years' service at age 18.
NATIONAL FLAG
 Horizontal stripes of red, white and blue; and the treasury seal in the center of the reverse side.
OFFICIAL LANGUAGE
 Spanish
COMBAT EFFECTIVENESS
 Limited
SPECIAL NOTES
 Military assumed control in 1954 and do so today. In 1977, a constitutional change will be required if General Stroessner seeks a sixth-term.

PERU

Defense Budget	$ 340,000,000
Population	16,333,000
Manpower in the Armed Forces	56,000
Defense as % of GNP	3.6%

ARMY

MANPOWER
    39,000 men

GENERAL
    Organized into 5 infantry brigades, 2 armored brigades, 1 commando and 1 jungle brigade. 1 paracommando unit, artillery and engineer battalions.

PRINCIPAL EQUIPMENT
    Weapons: 200 T-55 Tanks
                60 M-4 Tanks
                100 AMX-13 Tanks
                320 Armored Cars
                Light and Heavy Artillery
    Aircraft: 8 Bell 47s

NAVY

MANPOWER
    8,000 men

PRINCIPAL EQUIPMENT
    Vessels: 2 Cruisers
                6 Submarines
                4 Destroyers
                3 Destroyer Escorts
                2 Corvettes
                6 Fast Patrol Boats
                2 Coastal Minesweepers
                4 Landing Craft
                3 Coastal Patrol Boats
                7 River Gunboats
                3 Transports
                3 Oilers
                4 Frigates
    Aircraft: 6 Bell 47s
                2 Alouette IIIs
    Missiles: Seacat

AIR FORCE

MANPOWER
    9,000 men

PRINCIPAL EQUIPMENT
    Aircraft: Bombers   30 Canberras
                Fighters   14 Mirage Vs
                                    10 F-86Fs
                                     6 Hunters
                Fighter-Bombers   8 Mirage Vs
                                    24 IA-58 Pucara

Counter-Insurgency	24 Cessna A-37s
	40 T-41s
	20 T-33s
Reconnaissance	10 C-60s
	6 PV-2s
Transports	10 C-130s
	4 C-54s
	10 DH Doves
	18 Beech Queen Air
	15 DH Buffalo
	2 Learjets
Helicopters	7 Mi-6s
	4 Bell 47s
	10 Alouette IIIs
	13 Bell UH-1Ds
	9 Bell UH-1Hs
	17 Bell 212s

BASES
    La Palmas, Callao, Talara, Chiclayo, Iquitos, Piura, Pisco.

MISCELLANEOUS DATA

DEFENSE AGREEMENTS
    Rio Pact
MAP TYPE ASSISTANCE RECEIVED FROM
    U.S., U.S.S.R.
INTERNAL SECURITY FORCES
    18,000 men
CONSCRIPTION LAW
    2 years' compulsory service at age 21 to 25 -- only limited number drafted - followed by 5 years duty in reserve and then 20 years in National Guard.
NATIONAL FLAG
    Horizontal stripes of red, white and red with the national coat of arms in the center.
OFFICIAL LANGUAGE
    Spanish
COMBAT EFFECTIVENESS
    Limited
SPECIAL NOTES
    Peru's government has been under effective military control since 1968.
    Because of U.S. reluctance to furnish advanced jet fighters to Peru, they have threatened to procure MIG-21s from the U.S.S.R.

PHILIPPINES

Defense Budget	$ 165,000,000
Population	40,209,000
Manpower in the Armed Forces	55,000
Defense as % of GNP	1.5%

DEFENSE ESTABLISHMENT

The military establishment consists of the Army, Navy, Air Force and the Philippine Constabulary, subordinated and subject to the unified control of the Department of National Defense.

ARMY

MANPOWER
    35,000 men

GENERAL
    Country organized into four military areas geographically. Organization of tactical units is: 3 infantry divisions, 3 independent infantry brigades, 1 artillery group and 10 engineer battalions.

PRINCIPAL EQUIPMENT
    <u>Weapons</u>:   30 AMX-13, M-41 Tanks
                  25 Armored Personnel Carriers
                  Light and Heavy Artillery (in limited quantities)

NAVY

MANPOWER
    11,000 men (including Marines and engineers)

GENERAL
    As an island nation, Navy has important role in maintaining open sea lanes, executing amphibious operations, and ASW.

PRINCIPAL EQUIPMENT
    <u>Vessels</u>:   1 Destroyer Escort
                  9 Patrol Gunboats
                40 Patrol Craft
                4 Minesweepers
                11 Landing Ships
                4 Hydrofoils

AIR FORCE

MANPOWER
    9,000 men

PRINCIPAL EQUIPMENT
    <u>Aircraft</u>:   Fighter-Bombers   20 F-5s
                                    20 F-86s
                 Transports   28 C-47s
                                    8 F-27s
                                    4 C-130s
                                  15 C-123s

Helicopters	25 Bell UH-1s
	6 Hughes 300s
	5 H-34s
	2 S-62s
Light Tactical	32 SF-260Ws

BASES
    Pasay, Lipa City, Pampanga, Visayan, Zamboanga, Cubi Point

MISCELLANEOUS DATA

DEFENSE AGREEMENTS
    U.S.
MAP TYPE ASSISTANCE RECEIVED FROM
    U.S.
INTERNAL SECURITY FORCES
    Philippine Constabulary - 35,000
CONSCRIPTION LAW
    Selective service - chiefly volunteers.
MILITARY SCHOOLS
    Philippine Military Academy
NATIONAL FLAG
    Top half blue, bottom red, with a white triangle at the left containing a gold star in each corner and a golden sun in the center.
OFFICIAL LANGUAGE
    Filipino
COMBAT EFFECTIVENESS
    Limited
SPECIAL NOTES
    1972 martial law imposed on country.
    1973 new constitution established; martial law still in effect.
    Total reserves estimated at 300,000.

POLAND

Defense Budget	$ 2,230,000,000
Population	34,000,000
Manpower in the Armed Forces	330,000
Defense as % of GNP	5.3%

ARMY

MANPOWER
    185,000 men (Reserves of 800,000)

GENERAL
    Comprised of 5 armored, 1 amphibious assault, 8 mechanized infantry divisions, and 50 missile battalions.

PRINCIPAL EQUIPMENT

Weapons:
- 3,750 T-34/55/54/62 Tanks
- 300 PT-76 Tanks
- 1,700 Armored Personnel Carriers
- 125 Armored Cars
- 130 Scout Cars
- 700+ Pieces of Light Artillery
- 250+ Pieces of Medium Artillery
- 150+ Pieces of Heavy Artillery

Missiles:
- 50 Launchers w/Guideline
- Goa
- Frog
- Scud
- Snapper AT
- Swatter AT
- Sagger AT

NAVY

MANPOWER
    20,000 men (Reserves of 75,000) (1 Marine Battalion)

PRINCIPAL EQUIPMENT

Vessels:
- 5 Submarines
- 3 Destroyers
- 1 Destroyer w/SAMs
- 12 Guided Missile Patrol Boats
- 26 Sub Chasers
- 27 Minesweeping Launches
- 24 Fleet Minesweepers
- 20 Torpedo Boats
- 21 Landing Craft
- 38 Fast Patrol Boats
- 31 Support Vessels

Aircraft:
- 40 MIG-17s
- 9 IL-28s
- 10 Mi-1s
- 20 Mi-4s
- 3 Mi-2s

Missiles:
- Styx
- Samlet (for Coastal Defense)

AIR FORCE

MANPOWER
    55,000 men (Reserves of 110,000)
PRINCIPAL EQUIPMENT
    Aircraft:
	Bombers	30	Il-28s
	Fighter-Bombers	200+	MIG-17 and Su-7s
	Interceptors	250	MIG-17s
		48	MIG-19s
		150	MIG-21s
	Reconnaissance	48	MIG-21s
		22	Il-28s
	Helicopters	125+	Soviet Types
	Transports	54	An-2/12/24, IL-14/18/, Li-2s

    Missiles: SA-2
                  Atoll

MISCELLANEOUS DATA

DEFENSE AGREEMENTS
    Warsaw Pact
MAP TYPE ASSISTANCE RECEIVED FROM
    U.S.S.R.
INTERNAL SECURITY FORCES
    45,000 men
CONSCRIPTION LAW
    Compulsory service at age 20 - 2 years in Army or 3 years in Navy and Air Force.
NATIONAL FLAG
    Horizontal stripes of red and white.
OFFICIAL LANGUAGE
    Polish
COMBAT EFFECTIVENESS
    Excellent
SPECIAL NOTES
    2 Soviet divisions (tank) in Poland since 1964.

PORTUGAL

```
Defense Budget                  $ 686,000,000
Population                          8,740,000
Manpower in the Armed Forces          220,000
Defense as % of GNP                      7.8%
```

ARMY

MANPOWER
    179,000 men (Reserves of 550,000).
GENERAL
    Comprises 21 infantry, 2 tank, 7 artillery, 1 coast artillery, 3 AA, 7 cavalry, 3 engineer, 3 communications regiments; support units.
PRINCIPAL EQUIPMENT
    Weapons: M-4/41/47 Tanks
                  Armored Cars
                  Scout Cars
                  Armored Personnel Carriers
                  250+ Pieces of Artillery

NAVY

MANPOWER
    17,000 men (Reserves of 12,000)
      (Above includes 3,000 Marines)
PRINCIPAL EQUIPMENT
    Vessels: 8 Submarines
                  6 Corvettes
               12 Destroyer Escorts
               25 Coastal Patrol Vessels
                9 Coastal Minesweepers
                5 Oceangoing Minesweepers
               44 Patrol Launches
                1 Training Ship
                6 Survey Vessels
                5 Coast Guard Vessels
                2 River Gunboats
                2 Fleet Oilers
                1 Depot Ship
               57 Landing Craft
    Aircraft: 6 P-2s ASW Patrol

AIR FORCE

MANPOWER
    17,500 men (Reserves of 15,000)
PRINCIPAL EQUIPMENT
    Aircraft: Bombers   6 B-26s
                                        9 PV-2s
                  Fignter-Bombers 30 G-91s
                  Counter-
                    Insurgency   50 T-6s (armed)
                  Interceptors   23 F-86s

Transports	18 C-47s
	20 Noratlas
	10 DC-6s
	12 C-45s
	28 CASA-212s
Helicopters	100 Alouette IIIs
	25 Pumas

BASES
    Tanoas, Sintra, Porto, Montijo, Ota, Alverca, Jacinto.

MISCELLANEOUS DATA

DEFENSE AGREEMENTS
    NATO, Iberian Defense Alliance
MAP TYPE ASSISTANCE RECEIVED FROM
    U.S.
INTERNAL SECURITY FORCES
    15,000 men, plus Home Guard of over 500,000.
CONSCRIPTION LAW
    All males 21 to 45 subject to 18 months service in Air Force; 18 to 24 months in Army, or 48 months in Navy -- reserve duty until age 45.
NATIONAL FLAG
    Green and red vertical stripes, the red covering two-thirds of the flag; at the junction of the two is the national coat of arms in yellow, red and white.
OFFICIAL LANGUAGE
    Portugese
COMBAT EFFECTIVENESS
    Limited
SPECIAL NOTES
    In November of 1975, an attempted revolt was put down and the new government appears to be in hands of moderates in the military who seek transfer of government to civilian control.

QATAR

Defense Budget	N.A.
Population	180,000
Manpower in the Armed Forces	2,200
Defense as % of GNP	N.A.

ARMY

MANPOWER
   1,600 men

GENERAL
   Comprises 1 infantry regiment and 1 mobile regiment.

PRINCIPAL EQUIPMENT
   Weapons: Conventional
              30 Saladin Armored Cars
               8 Saracen Armored Cars
              10 Ferret Scout Cars
              Light Artillery
   Missiles: Vigilant AT

NAVY

None.

Army operates small fleet of 4 armed launches.

AIR FORCE

MANPOWER
   300 men

PRINCIPAL EQUIPMENT
   Aircraft: Fighter-Bombers   4 Hunters
               Helicopters   2 Whirlwinds
                                  2 Sea Kings
                                  2 Gazelles
   Missiles: Tigercat

MISCELLANEOUS DATA

DEFENSE AGREEMENTS
   U.K., Arab League, United Arab Emirates

MAP TYPE ASSISTANCE RECEIVED FROM
   U.K.

INTERNAL SECURITY FORCES
   500 men

CONSCRIPTION LAW
   Volunteer forces

NATIONAL FLAG
   Maroon with serrated border on hoist.

OFFICIAL LANGUAGE
   Arabic

Defense Budget $ 94,000,000
Population   5,775,000
Manpower in the Armed Forces   4,600
Defense as % of GNP   3.2%

ARMY

MANPOWER
 3,500 men (Reserves of 25,000)
GENERAL
 Organized into 2 infantry battalions, 1 air unit, and 1 artillery battery, support units.
PRINCIPAL EQUIPMENT
 Weapons: 20 Ferret Scout Cars
             Conventional Arms
             Light Artillery

NAVY

None.

AIR FORCE

MANPOWER
 1,200 men (Reserves of 500)
PRINCIPAL EQUIPMENT
 Aircraft: Bombers   9 Canberras
             Fighter-Bombers   12 Hunters
                                  9 Vampires
             Reconnaissance   12 Provosts
             Transports   3 C-47s
                                  1 Baron
             Helicopters   8 Alouette IIIs
             Armed Trainers   10 Provosts
                                  7 AL-60s

MISCELLANEOUS DATA

DEFENSE AGREEMENTS
 Informal only.
MAP TYPE ASSISTANCE RECEIVED FROM
 U.K.
INTERNAL SECURITY FORCES
 7,400 men, plus police reserve of 28,500)
CONSCRIPTION LAW
 All males may be required to serve 12 months.
NATIONAL FLAG
 Three equal stripes running vertically of green, white and green, with the Rhodesian coat of arms centered on the white stripe.
OFFICIAL LANGUAGE
 English
COMBAT EFFECTIVENESS
 Limited

RUMANIA

Defense Budget	$ 790,000,000
Population	20,470,000
Manpower in the Armed Forces	179,000
Defense as % of GNP	3%

ARMY

MANPOWER
 150,000 men (Reserves of 250,000)
GENERAL
 The Romanian People's Army comprises all of the regular armed forces administered by the Ministry of the Armed Forces.
 There are 3 military regions and 3 army corps; with 3 motorized infantry divisions and supporting tank, artillery, engineer and recon units. Also, 2 tank divisions at Bucharest and Lipova, 2 mountain divisions at Tirgu Mures and Sinaia, 2 motorized divisions and 1 artillery division at Tecuci. Artillery has 14 regiments.
PRINCIPAL EQUIPMENT
 <u>Weapons</u>: 2,000 Tanks - T-34, T-54, T-55s
    50 Tanks - T-62
  1,000 Armored Personnel Carriers
  Light and Heavy Artillery
 <u>Missiles</u>: Frog
  Scud
  Sagger
  Snapper
  Swatter

NAVY

MANPOWER
 9,000 men (Reserves of 10,000)
GENERAL
 Almost 200 vessels, but old and with little capability outside coast line and definitely not beyond the Black Sea.
PRINCIPAL EQUIPMENT
 <u>Ships</u>: 3 Coastal Escorts
  5 Missile Boats
  8 Motor Torpedo Boats
  3 Patrol Vessels
  4 Minesweepers
  22 Inshore Minesweepers
  3 Training Ships
  8 Minesweeping Boats
  25 Service Craft
 <u>Aircraft</u>: 4 Mi-4 Helicopters
 <u>Missiles</u>: Styx

AIR FORCE

MANPOWER
 20,000 men (Reserves of 22,000)

GENERAL
 Commander of air and air defense forces reports to Minister of Armed Forces.

PRINCIPAL EQUIPMENT

Aircraft:	Interceptors	3 Fighter Regiments MIG-21s
	Ground Attack	2 regiments with MIG-17 and 19s
	Transports	3 Squadrons with 8 Il-14s 4 Li-2s 4 An-24s
	Helicopters	10 Mi-1, Mi-4, Mi-8s, Alouette IIIs
Missiles:	Guideline Atoll	

MISCELLANEOUS DATA

DEFENSE AGREEMENTS
 Warsaw Pact

MAP TYPE ASSISTANCE RECEIVED FROM
 U.S.S.R.

INTERNAL SECURITY FORCES
 50,000 men (Militia with 500,000)

CONSCRIPTION LAW
 Compulsory service: 16 months in Army, 2 years in Navy or Air Force. All are in Reserve until age 50.

MILITARY SCHOOLS
 General Military Academy, Military Technical Academy, Naval School at Constanta.

NATIONAL FLAG
 Blue, yellow, red (vertical), with the coat of arms of the republic in the middle.

OFFICIAL LANGUAGE
 Rumanian

COMBAT EFFECTIVENESS
 Limited

SPECIAL NOTES
 Although part of Warsaw Pact, they allowed status of forces agreement with U.S.S.R. to lapse.
 Army has been developing relations with socialist countries in Europe, Asia and Latin America.
 Rumania openly denounced invasion of Czechoslovakia in 1968 and did not participate in it.

RWANDA

```
Defense Budget                 $ 8,000,000
Population                       4,200,000
Manpower in the Armed Forces         3,750
Defense as % of GNP                   4.0%
```

ARMY

MANPOWER
   3,750 men

GENERAL
   Organized into motorized infantry battalions, reconnaissance squadron, parachute company.

PRINCIPAL EQUIPMENT
   Weapons: 10 M-8 Armored Cars
               4 M-20 Armored Cars
              Mortars
   Aircraft: 1 Do-27 Transport
              2 Alouette II Helicopters
              3 Fouga Magisters
              2 C-47 Transports

Rwanda has no Navy or Air Force -- aircraft are flown by Army Personnel.

MISCELLANEOUS DATA

DEFENSE AGREEMENTS
   Equatorial Defense Council

MAP TYPE ASSISTANCE RECEIVED FROM
   Belgium

INTERNAL SECURITY FORCES
   650 men

CONSCRIPTION LAW
   Volunteer forces

NATIONAL FLAG
   Vertical stripes of red, yellow and green with a black "R" in the center.

OFFICIAL LANGUAGE
   Rwanda and French

COMBAT EFFECTIVENESS
   Limited

SPECIAL NOTES
   Military coup overthrew government in 1973 and since that time a civil-military government has prevailed.

Defense Budget	$ 100,000 (estimated)
Population	18,831
Manpower in the Armed Forces	Militia Only
Defense as % of GNP	N.A.

ARMY

MANPOWER
   85 men

San Marino has no formal armed forces per se. It has a Noble Guard for ceremonial purposes only. There is also a small force, Guardia di Rocca, for border patrol purposes.

MISCELLANEOUS DATA

DEFENSE AGREEMENTS
   Italy
INTERNAL SECURITY FORCES
   35 men
CONSCRIPTION LAW
   All citizens 16 to 55 with the exception of teachers and students, must serve in the militia in times of emergency.
NATIONAL FLAG
   Horizontal stripes of white and blue with the national coat of arms in the center.
OFFICIAL LANGUAGE
   Italian
SPECIAL NOTES
   San Marino is not a member of the UN; but maintains an Observer at the UN office in Geneva.

SAUDI ARABIA

Defense Budget	$ 6,000,000,000
Population	8,000,000
Manpower in the Armed Forces	51,000
Defense as % of GNP	21%

DEFENSE ESTABLISHMENT

The King, as chief of state, is Commander-in-Chief of the Armed Forces. Under him is a Minister of Defense and Aviation.

The Minister of Defense and Aviation exercises supervision and operational control over the army, the navy and the air force as well as control of all civil aviation.

The National Guard is under the personal control of the King through a commander personally appointed by him.

Within the Ministry of Defense and Aviation, a chief of staff is directly responsible to the minister for the supervision of all forces.

ARMY

MANPOWER
   40,000 men
GENERAL
   Country is divided into nine area commands. Army is organized into four infantry brigades, 11 battalions (1 armored, 2 recon., 1 parachute, 3 artillery, 3 AA, and the Royal Guards).
   Largest garrisons are at: Jidda, Dammam, Taif, Al-Khar and Riyadh.
PRINCIPAL EQUIPMENT
   Weapons: Est. 300 Tanks (M-47, AMX-30s)*
              Est. 200+ AML 60/90 Armored Cars
              Light Artillery
   Missiles: Hawk

NAVY

MANPOWER
   1,500 men
GENERAL
   Coast Guard duties only.
PRINCIPAL EQUIPMENT
   Vessels: 22 Patrol Boats
              8 SRN-6 Hovercraft
              4 Fast Patrol Boats

* 500 Tanks on order.

AIR FORCE

MANPOWER
 10,000 men
GENERAL
 Small and being updated rapidly.
PRINCIPAL EQUIPMENT
<u>Aircraft</u>: Fighter-Bombers   65 F-5s*
　　　　　　　Interceptors   35 BAC Lightnings
　　　　　　　　　　　　　　　 38 Mirage IIIs
　　　　　　　Ground Attack   27 BAC 167s
　　　　　　　Transports   30 C-130s
　　　　　　　　　　　　　　　　2 C-140s
　　　　　　　Helicopters   22 Bell 206s
　　　　　　　　　　　　　　　 10 Bell 205s
　<u>Missiles</u>: Thunderbird
BASES
 Ridyah, Jeddah, Taif, Yanbu, Dhahran, Tabuk, Khamia Mushayt, Jizan, Mejran.

MISCELLANEOUS DATA

DEFENSE AGREEMENTS
 Arab League Collective Security Pact, Jordan
MAP TYPE ASSISTANCE RECEIVED FROM
 U.K., U.S.
INTERNAL SECURITY FORCES
 30,000 men
CONSCRIPTION LAW
 Volunteer forces
MILITARY SCHOOLS
 Royal Military College, Military Preparatory School, Numerous Technical Institutes
NATIONAL FLAG
 Green, with white crossed swords and the text "There is but one God and Mohammed is his prophet" in white Arabic characters.
OFFICIAL LANGUAGE
 Arabic
COMBAT EFFECTIVENESS
 Excellent

* 50 on order.

SENEGAL

Defense Budget	$ 21,000,000
Population	4,120,500
Manpower in the Armed Forces	7,500
Defense as % of GNP	2.6%

ARMY

MANPOWER
    6,500 men (Reserves of 10,000)
GENERAL
    Organized into 4 motorized infantry battalions of 5 companies each; paratroop, commando and engineer units.
PRINCIPAL EQUIPMENT
    Weapons: Conventional
                Armored Cars AML-425, M-8s
                Light Artillery

NAVY

MANPOWER
    175 men
PRINCIPAL EQUIPMENT
    Vessels: 3 Patrol Boats
                2 Landing Craft

AIR FORCE

MANPOWER
    300 men
PRINCIPAL EQUIPMENT
    Aircraft: Transports   4 C-47s
                                4 Broussards
                Helicopters   2 Bell 47s
                                2 Alouette IIs

MISCELLANEOUS DATA

DEFENSE AGREEMENTS
    Equatorial Defense Council, Fránce
INTERNAL SECURITY FORCES
    1,600 men
CONSCRIPTION LAW
    Volunteer forces
NATIONAL FLAG
    Vertical stripes of green, yellow and red, with a green star in the center.
OFFICIAL LANGUAGE
    French
COMBAT EFFECTIVENESS
    Limited

Defense Budget	$ 4,000,000
Population	2,678,000
Manpower in the Armed Forces	2,500
Defense as % of GNP	0.9%

ARMY

MANPOWER
   1,800 men

GENERAL
   Organized into 1 infantry battalion, 1 armored car squadron, 1 signal squadron, plus support units.

PRINCIPAL EQUIPMENT
   Weapons: Conventional
              Armored Cars

   Sierra Leone has no Navy or Air Force per se. These functions are provided by units of the Army.

   About 70 men operate 2 motor launches and 1 patrol boat, and 1 patrol gunboat. There are also two liaison type aircraft.

MISCELLANEOUS DATA

MAP TYPE ASSISTANCE RECEIVED FROM
   Nigeria, U.K.

INTERNAL SECURITY FORCES
   2,900 men

CONSCRIPTION LAW
   Volunteer forces

NATIONAL FLAG
   Horizontal stripes of green, white and blue.

OFFICIAL LANGUAGE
   English

COMBAT EFFECTIVENESS
   Limited

SINGAPORE

Defense Budget	$ 215,000,000
Population	2,186,000
Manpower in the Armed Forces	16,000
Defense as % of GNP	9%

ARMY

MANPOWER
 14,000 men (Reserves of 30,000)
GENERAL
 Organized into 4 brigades: 1 armored and 3 infantry with 1 tank, 2 mechanized, 9 infantry, 3 artillery, 3 engineer and 1 signal battalions.
PRINCIPAL EQUIPMENT
 Weapons: 80 AMX-13 Tanks
  M-706 Armored Personnel Carriers
  Light Artillery

NAVY

MANPOWER
 1,000 men (Reserves of 500)
PRINCIPAL EQUIPMENT
 Vessels: 2 Seaward Defense Boats
  9 Patrol Boats (Gabriel SSM)
  1 Landing Ship
  4 Landing Craft
  3 Miscellaneous Small Craft

AIR FORCE

MANPOWER
 2,500 men
PRINCIPAL EQUIPMENT
 Aircraft: Fighter-Bombers 40 A-4 Skyhawks
   20 Hunters
  Counter-Insurgency 15 BAC-167s
   14 SF-260s
  Transports 6 Skyvans
   8 Cessna 170s
   2 Airtourer
  Helicopters 8 Alouette IIIs
 Missiles: Rapier
  Bloodhound

MISCELLANEOUS DATA

DEFENSE AGREEMENTS
 Australia, New Zealand
MAP TYPE ASSISTANCE RECEIVED FROM
 U.K., Australia, Israel

INTERNAL SECURITY FORCES
    1,300 men
CONSCRIPTION LAW
    2 years' compulsory service age 18 to 45; reserve duty for 10 years or to age 40.
NATIONAL FLAG
    Horizontal stripes of red and white with a white crescent.
OFFICIAL LANGUAGE
    Malay
COMBAT EFFECTIVENESS
    Limited

SOMALIA

Defense Budget	$ 16,000,000
Population	2,930,000
Manpower in the Armed Forces	25,750
Defense as % of GNP	7.0%

DEFENSE ESTABLISHMENT

The President is designated as the commander-in-chief of Somalian armed forces. The Minister of Defense operates through a High Command group which exercises operational control over commanders of the separate services.

ARMY

MANPOWER
  20,000 men
GENERAL
  Organized into battalions: 6 tank, 9 mechanized infantry, 2 commando, 5 field artiller, and 5 anti-aircraft battalions.
PRINCIPAL EQUIPMENT
  Weapons: Est. 225 T-34/54/55 Tanks
            Est. 350 Armored Personnel Carriers
            Est. 100 Pieces of Artillery (76mm up)

NAVY

MANPOWER
  250 men
PRINCIPAL EQUIPMENT
  Vessels: 6 Motor Torpedo Boats
            2 Coastal Escorts

AIR FORCE

MANPOWER
  5,500 men
PRINCIPAL EQUIPMENT
  Aircraft: Fighter-Bombers   30 MIG-21s
                              19 MIG-17s
                               6 MIG-19s
            Light Bombers   4 Il-28s
            Transports   3 An-24s
                               3 An-2s
                               3 C-47s
                               8 P-148s
            Helicopters   12 Mi-4/8s
BASES
  Mogadishu, Hargeisa, and multiple strips.

MISCELLANEOUS DATA

DEFENSE AGREEMENTS
   U.S.S.R.
MAP TYPE ASSISTANCE RECEIVED FROM
   U.S.S.R., UAR, Yugoslavia, U.K.
INTERNAL SECURITY FORCES
   Somali Police Force 3,500, Border Guard 500, People's Militia 3,000.
CONSCRIPTION LAW
   Volunteer forces
MILITARY SCHOOLS
   Somali Army Officer's Academy
NATIONAL FLAG
   Blue shield with a 5-pointed white star in the center.
OFFICIAL LANGUAGE
   Arabic, Italian, and English
COMBAT EFFECTIVENESS
   Limited
SPECIAL NOTES
   1969, the President was assassinated and army assumed power.
   1970, a counter revolutionary plot was quelled.
   Soviet landing fields and naval bases have been established on the horn of Africa (Somalia).
   Soviet pilots have been reported flying MIG-21 aircraft in country.
   Ethiopia has expressed concern to the UN relative to Somalian aggressiveness in border disputes.

SOUTH AFRICA

Defense Budget	$ 1,037,000,000
Population	21,534,000
Manpower in the Armed Forces	54,000
Defense as % of GNP	16%

ARMY

MANPOWER
      32,000 men

GENERAL
      Country divided into 11 commands: Regular Force, Citizen Force and Kommandos probably number about 120,000 trained personnel.

PRINCIPAL EQUIPMENT
      Weapons: 200 Tanks - Centurion, M-4, Comets
                  1000 Armored Cars - AMX-60/90s
                  250 Ferret Scout Cars
                  200 Saracen Armored Personnel Carriers
                  150 Commando Armored Personnel Carriers
                  Light and Medium Artillery
      Aircraft: 34 U-17s
                  40 Aeromacchi AM3s
                  8 Alouette IIIs

NAVY

MANPOWER
      4,000 men

PRINCIPAL EQUIPMENT
      Vessels: 4 Frigates (with Gabriel Missiles)
                  6 Submarines
                  2 Destroyers (with Wasp Helicopters)
                  6 ASW Destroyers
                  10 Coastal Minesweepers
                  2 Training Frigates
                  1 Survey Vessel
                  2 Boom Defense Vessels
                  6 Seaward Defense Boats
                  1 Fast Replenishment Ship
                  5 Submarine Chasers
      Helicopters: 17 Wasps
                  12 Alouette II/IIIs

AIR FORCE

MANPOWER
      8,000 men

PRINCIPAL EQUIPMENT
      Aircraft: Fighter-Bombers   48 Mirage F-1s
                  Strike   100 MB.326s
                                     18 Mirage IIIs
                  ASW Patrol   7 Shackletons
                                     18 Piaggio P-166s

Bombers	6	Canberras
	10	Buccaneers
Counter-Insurgency	150	MB.326s
Reconnaissance	25	Mirage IIIs
Transports	7	C-130s
	9	Transalls
	20	C-47s
	5	C-54s
	1	Viscount
	4	HS-125s
Helicopters	40	Alouette IIIs
	20	Pumas
	15	Super Frelons

Missiles: AS-20
AS-30
MATRA
Crotale
Sidewinder

BASES
    Dunottar, Pietersberg, Waterkloof, Swartkop, Durban, Ysterplaat, Bloemfontein, Bleomspruit, Grand Central, Potchefstromm, Pt. Elizabeth, Youngsfield, D.F. Malan, Langebaanweg.

MISCELLANEOUS DATA

MAP TYPE ASSISTANCE RECEIVED FROM
    Canada, France, Switzerland, U.K., U.S., West Germany.
INTERNAL SECURITY FORCES
    112,000 men
CONSCRIPTION LAW
    2 years' compulsory service.
NATIONAL FLAG
    Horizontal stripes of orange, white and blue with small replicas of the Union Jack, the old flag of the Orange Free State, and old Transvaal Vierkleur banner in the center.
OFFICIAL LANGUAGE
    English and Afrikaans
COMBAT EFFECTIVENESS
    Excellent
SPECIAL NOTES
    South Africa's apartheid policy has created conditions in which most Western nations who were previous arms suppliers are reluctant to continue sales to this country; and, as a result, it has moved deeply into aircraft, shipbuilding, and arms production internally.

SPAIN

Defense Budget	$ 1,650,000,000
Population	34,879,000
Manpower in the Armed Forces	293,600
Defense as % of GNP	5.2%

ARMY

MANPOWER
    210,000 men

GENERAL
    Organized divisions: 1 armored, 2 motorized infantry, 2 mountain; 14 infantry brigades, 2 artillery brigades, 1 parachute brigade, 1 armored cavalry brigade and 2 missile battalions.

PRINCIPAL EQUIPMENT

Weapons:
- 250 M-24/41 Tanks
- 200 AMX-30 Tanks
- 300+ M-47/48 Tanks
- 60 M-113 Armored Personnel Carriers
-     Armored Cars/Scout Cars
- 300 Pieces Light, Medium Artillery
- 50 Pieces of Heavy Artillery

Aircraft:
- 30 CASA 127 Liaison
- 10 Bell 47s
- 12 UH-1Bs
- 6 CH-47s
- 16 Bell 206s
- 15 UH-1s

Missiles:
- Hawk
- Nike-Hercules

NAVY

MANPOWER
    51,000 men

PRINCIPAL EQUIPMENT

Vessels:
- 1 Cruiser
- 23 Destroyers
- 1 Helicopter Carrier
- 8 Submarines
- 9 Frigates (6 w/Missiles)
- 6 Frigate Minelayers
- 20 Minesweepers
- 3 ASW Patrol Vessels
- 6 Corvettes
- 3 Motor Torpedo Boats
- 1 Training Ship
- 3 Survey Vessels
- 1 River Patrol Boat
- 11 Landing Craft
- 4 Oilers
- 3 Transports
- 2 Tenders
- 1 Boom Defense

Helicopters:	6 SH-3s	
	8 Bell 204s	
	9 H-19s	
	5 Hughes 500s	
	3 Sikorsky CH-47s	
Aircraft:	8 Harriers	

AIR FORCE

MANPOWER
    32,600 men
PRINCIPAL EQUIPMENT

Aircraft:	ASW Patrol	11 SA-16s
	Fighter-Bombers	21 Mirage F-1s
		36 F-4s
		24 Mirage IIIs
		40 HA-200s Saeta
		25 Super Saetas
	Transports	10 DH Caribous
		24 C-47s
		9 C-54s
		20 CASA 207s
		6 C-130s
		32 Aviocars
	Helicopters	8 CH-47s
		8 OH-58s
		20 Bell 47s
		8 Bell 206s
		- Bell 205s
Missiles:	Sidewinder	
	Matra	

BASES
    Valencia, Zaragoza, Seville, Madrid (3), Malaga, Valladolid, Jerez, Albacete, Las Palmas, Guinea, Majorca, Murcia, Granada, Salamanca, Badajoz, Murcia, La Parra, Los Alcazares.

MISCELLANEOUS DATA

DEFENSE AGREEMENTS
    Joint Iberian Defense Alliance
MAP TYPE ASSISTANCE RECEIVED FROM
    U.S.
INTERNAL SECURITY FORCES
    65,000 men
CONSCRIPTION LAW
    Compulsory service: 16 months in Army, 24 months in Navy, and 18 months in Air Force.
NATIONAL FLAG
    Horizontal stripes of red, yellow, red with the Spanish coat of arms in the center.
OFFICIAL LANGUAGE
    Spanish
COMBAT EFFECTIVENESS
    Excellent
SPECIAL NOTES
    U.S. armed forces have base rights in Rota for U.S. Navy and the USAF has use of air bases near Seville and Madrid and Zaragoza.

SRI LANKA

Defense Budget	$ 25,000,000
Population	12,747,000
Manpower in the Armed Forces	12,300
Defense as % of GNP	2.1%

DEFENSE ESTABLISHMENT

The Prime Minister is constitutionally required to serve as the Minister of Defense adn External Affairs. The armed forces are organized into three branches: Army, Navy and Air Force.

ARMY

MANPOWER
  8,000 men (Reserves of 6,000)
GENERAL
  The Army is basically an infantry force, organized into brigades with three battalions each.
PRINCIPAL EQUIPMENT
  Weapons: 6 Armored Cars
             20 Armored Personnel Carriers
             Light Artillery

NAVY

MANPOWER
  2,400 men
GENERAL
  Main role purely coastal patrol
PRINCIPAL EQUIPMENT
  Ships: 1 Frigate
             27 Patrol Boats
             1 Hydrofoil

AIR FORCE

MANPOWER
  1,900 men (Reserves of 2,000)
GENERAL
  Primary mission is to assist anti-smuggling operations of Navy and air support to Army in its internal security operations.
PRINCIPAL EQUIPMENT
  Aircraft: 5 MIG-17s
             4 H.S. Doves
             4 H.S. Herons
             4 Cessna 337s
             1 Convair 440
             5 Bell 47G Helicopters
             7 Bell 206A Helicopters
             2 Kamov Ka-26 Helicopters

MISCELLANEOUS DATA

DEFENSE AGREEMENTS
   Government opposes all military alliances.
MAP TYPE ASSISTANCE RECEIVED FROM
   U.K., U.S.S.R., U.S.
INTERNAL SECURITY FORCES
   15,000 men
CONSCRIPTION LAW
   Volunteer forces
MILITARY SCHOOLS
   Officers trained in foreign military schools.
NATIONAL FLAG
   Narrow green and orange vertical stripes on the left side, with a yellow lion carrying a sword in one upraised paw against a red background occupying the rest of the flag. Entire flag bordered in yellow, with a vertical yellow band separating the orange and green stripes from the red background of the rest of the flag.
OFFICIAL LANGUAGE
   Ceylonese or Sinhalese
COMBAT EFFECTIVENESS
   Limited

SUDAN, REP. OF

Defense Budget	$ 611,000,000
Population	17,000,000
Manpower in the Armed Forces	43,100
Defense as % of GNP	4.0%

DEFENSE ESTABLISHMENT

The armed forces are organized under the Ministry of Defense. Headquarters are in Khartoum.

ARMY

MANPOWER
40,000 men

GENERAL
The country is organized into six commands - the Army has seven infantry, two armored, one parachute brigade, three artillery, three air defense and one engineer regiment.

PRINCIPAL EQUIPMENT
Weapons: Est. 150 T-34/54/55/62 Tanks
           Est. 100 Armored Cars
           Est. 200 Armored Personnel Carriers
           Est. 100 Artillery Pieces over 105mm
           Light Artillery
Missiles: Hawk

NAVY

MANPOWER
600 men

GENERAL
Coast Guard duties only. Formed in 1962.

PRINCIPAL EQUIPMENT
Vessels: 6 Patrol Boats
           2 Landing Craft
           1 Oiler
           1 Water Carrier
           1 Survey Vessel

AIR FORCE

MANPOWER
2,500 men

GENERAL
Being restructured and re-equipped with Soviet aid.

PRINCIPAL EQUIPMENT
Aircraft: Fighter-Bombers   24 MIG-21s
                             17 MIG-17s
           Transports   3 Pembrokes
                              6 An-12s
                              5 An-24s
                              2 C-47s

SUDAN, REP. OF

        Armed Trainers   5 BAC-145s
                                  5 Provost Mk-55s
        Helicopters   15 Mi-4/8s

BASES
    Khartoum, Wadi Halfa, Wadi Seidna, Juba, and local air strips.

MISCELLANEOUS DATA

DEFENSE AGREEMENTS
    Arab League
MAP TYPE ASSISTANCE RECEIVED FROM
    UAR, U.S., U.S.S.R., W. Germany, Yugoslavia
INTERNAL SECURITY FORCES
    4,500 Border Guards, 500 National Guard
CONSCRIPTION LAW
    Volunteer Forces
MILITARY SCHOOLS
    Military College, Sudanese Staff College
NATIONAL FLAG
    Black, white, red (horizontal) with green triangle at the masthead.
OFFICIAL LANGUAGE
    Arabic
COMBAT EFFECTIVENESS
    Limited, but increasingly being improved

SWEDEN

Defense Budget	$ 1,884,000,000
Population	8,208,000
Manpower in the Armed Forces	28,400 (Cadre only)
Defense as % of GNP	3.7%

ARMY

MANPOWER
    18,000 men (8,000 cadre, 10,000 reservists) (Reserves of over 100,000 receive annual 3 to 4 week refresher training)

GENERAL
    Ground forces consist of standing Army "on leave", but can be mobilized on short notice. Regulars are "cadre" troops with conscript trainees and reservists called up for 18 to 40 day periods annually.
    Army comprises 20 infantry, 6 armored, 4 Norrland brigades, and about 50 independent infantry, artillery and AA battalions. On mobilization, they can field equivalent of 15 combat divisions.

PRINCIPAL EQUIPMENT
    Weapons: 300 Centurion Tanks
                     Strv-S Tanks
                     1KV-91 Tank Destroyers
                     Strv-74 Light Tanks
                     Armored Personnel Carriers
                     Light and Heavy Artillery
    Missiles: TOW AT
                     Hawk
                     Redeye

NAVY

MANPOWER
    4,700 men (3,000 reservists and 7,500 conscripts) (About 7,000 conscripts receive annual refresher training).

PRINCIPAL EQUIPMENT
    Vessels: 1 Cruiser
                     6 Destroyers (with missiles)
                     2 Destroyers
                     6 ASW Frigates
                     20 Submarines
                     45 Motor Torpedo Boats
                     20 Patrol Launches
                     9 Minelayers
                     10 Mine Tenders
                     17 Coastal Minesweepers
                     15 Inshore Minesweepers
                     70 Landing Craft
                     39 Auxiliaries
    Weapons: 5 Coast Defense Artillery Regiments with medium and heavy artillery and SSMs

    Aircraft: 30 Helicopters (Alouette II/Vertol 107/
                      AB-206s)
    Missiles: Seacat
                 Penguin

AIR FORCE

MANPOWER
    5,700 men (2,000 reservices, 6,300 conscripts)
  About 6,000 conscripts on annual refresher training.
PRINCIPAL EQUIPMENT

Aircraft:	Fighter-Bombers	76	SAAB A-32s
		36	SAAB A-37s
		20	SAAB Sk-60s
	Interceptors	315	SAAB J-35/JA-37s
	Reconnaissance	45	SAAB J-35s
		40	SAAB J-32s
	Transports	4	C-130s
		7	C-47s
		6	Norseman
		10	Pembroke
	Helicopters	10	Vertol 107s
			Alouette II/IIIs
			Bell 204/206s
Missiles:	Bloodhound		
	Falcon		
	Sidewinder		
	Robot		

BASES
    Haslo, Ljunghyed, Ostersund, Karlsborg, Satenas, Angelholm, Nykoping, Kalmar, Norrkoping, Uppsala, Kallinge, Blekinge, Tullinge, Lulea, Halmstad, Malmstaff.

MISCELLANEOUS DATA

DEFENSE AGREEMENTS
    None, in light of strict neutrality posture.
MAP TYPE ASSISTANCE RECEIVED FROM
    None, in light of strict neutrality posture.
INTERNAL SECURITY FORCES
    300,000 men
CONSCRIPTION LAW
    Compulsory service: 9-15 months in Army and Navy or 9-14 months in Air Force.
NATIONAL FLAG
    An extended yellow cross on a blue field.
OFFICIAL LANGUAGE
    Swedish
combat effectiveness
    Excellent
SPECIAL NOTES
    Sweden maintains a neutral role and is the most active government in urging arms control progress. Sweden is the first nation to allocate 1% of its GNP to foreign economic aid.

SWITZERLAND

Defense Budget $890,000,000
Population 6,438,000
Manpower in the Armed Forces 6,500 Regulars
36,000 Conscript Trainees
Defense as % of GNP 5%

ARMY

MANPOWER
   3,500 Regulars, 30,000 Conscript Trainees
     (Reserves of 550,000, mobilizable in 24 hours)

GENERAL
   1 mountain corps with 3 infantry divisions; 3 plateau region corps with 1 mechanized, 1 infantry, and 1 frontier division; 23 independent brigades.

PRINCIPAL EQUIPMENT
   Weapons: 625 Centurion, Pz-61/68 Tanks
               200 AMX-13 Tanks
               1250 Armored Personnel Carriers
               Light and Heavy Artillery
   Vessels: 4 Patrol Boats for major lakes
   Missiles: Oerlikon

NAVY

None.

AIR FORCE

MANPOWER
   3,000 Regulars, 6,000 Conscript Trainees, (Reserves of 45,000)

PRINCIPAL EQUIPMENT
   Aircraft: Fighter-Bombers   150 DH Venom
               Interceptors   126 HS Hunters
                                   38 Mirage IIIs
               Reconnaissance   30 Mirage IIIs
               Transports   3 Ju-52s
                                    3 Twin Bonanza
                                   12 Pilatus Porter
               Liaison   30 Do-27s
               Helicopters   55 Alouette II/IIIs
   Missiles: Bloodhound
               Hughes HM-558
               Sidewinder
               AS-30
               Bantam AT

BASES
   Dubendorf, Emmen, Payerne, Meiringen, Locarno, Sion, plus strips.

MISCELLANEOUS DATA

DEFENSE AGREEMENTS
   None... policy of strict neutrality.

MAP TYPE ASSISTANCE RECEIVED FROM
   None.

INTERNAL SECURITY FORCES
   See Special Notes below.

CONSCRIPTION LAW
   Compulsory service for all males between 20 and 50. Four months of basic training, followed by 3 weeks annual reserve training for 8 years. Then, 2 weeks annual training for 3 years, and finally, 1 weeks training for 2 years.

NATIONAL FLAG
   A red field with a white cross in the center.

OFFICIAL LANGUAGE
   German, French and Italian.

COMBAT EFFECTIVENESS
   Excellent

SPECIAL NOTES
   The entire national militia can be mobilized in 48 hours. Fortifications throughout the country are extensive - all international tunnels, main entry passes, etc. are prepared for demolition on an "immediate at-ready basis".

   Switzerland is not a member of the UN, but does maintain Observer status.

   Switzerland handles diplomatic, defense and customs functions for Liechtenstein.

SYRIA

Defense Budget	$ 500,000,000
Population	7,000,000
Manpower in the Armed Forces	143,700
Defense as % of GNP	14%

ARMY

MANPOWER
 130,000 men (Reserves of 200,000)

GENERAL
 Organized into 4 armored, 3 infantry divisions; 3 mechanized, 1 infantry, 2 artillery, 6 commando brigades. Est. 35 SAM batteries.

PRINCIPAL EQUIPMENT
- Weapons:
  - 750 T-62 Tanks
  - 15 JS-3 Tanks
  - 1200 T-34 Tanks
  - 800 T-54, T-55, T-62 Tanks
  - 75 PT-76 Tanks
  - Light and Heavy Artillery (est. 1300 pcs.)
  - 1200 Armored Personnel Carriers
- Missiles:
  - Guideline
  - Goa
  - Scud B
  - Strela

NAVY

MANPOWER
 1,700 men (Reserves of 3,500)

GENERAL
 Navy is under control of Army.

PRINCIPAL EQUIPMENT
- Ships:
  - 3 Minesweepers
  - 3 Coastal Patrol Vessels
  - 15 MTBs
  - 8 Missile Boats
- Missiles: Styx SSM

AIR FORCE

MANPOWER
 12,000 men

GENERAL
 Operates over 500 combat aircraft out of 14 bases.

PRINCIPAL EQUIPMENT
- Aircraft:
  - Fighter-Bombers
    - 36 MIG-21s
    - 45 MIG-23s
    - 30 Su-7s
    - 75 MIG-17s
  - Fighters
    - 200 MIG-21s
    - 36 Mirage Vs
    - 40 MIG-28s
    - 12 MIG-25s

Bombers	10 Il-28s
Transports	3 An-24s
	30 An-12s
	40 Il-14s
Helicopters	35 Mi-4s
	20 Mi-6s
	70 Mi-8s
	19 Westland Commando
	6 Westland Sea Kings

Missiles: Guideline SAM
Atoll AAM
Goa SAM
Gainful SAM
Strela SAM

MISCELLANEOUS DATA

DEFENSE AGREEMENTS
   Arab League Collective Security Pact
MAP TYPE ASSISTANCE RECEIVED FROM
   U.S.S.R., N. Korea, UAR
INTERNAL SECURITY FORCES
   8,000 Gendarmerie, 1,500 Desert Guards
CONSCRIPTION LAW
   Compulsory service for 30 months. Upon completion of tour of duty, placed in reserve for 18 years; after which they revert to inactive status.
MILITARY SCHOOLS
   The Military Academy, The Naval Academy, The Air Force Academy
NATIONAL FLAG
   Horizontal stripes of red, white, black, with three green stars in the center
OFFICIAL LANGUAGE
   Arabic
SPECIAL NOTES
   Almost all military training is in hands of Soviet instructors.
   Almost $500-million in military equipment aid has been given Syria by the USSR in past two years.
   Present government is result of military coup in February, 1966. President is Lieut. General Hafez al Assad.
   Syria has been the most positive aid to Arab guerrillas operating in Israel providing training, weapons and supplies.
   There is a Cuban brigade of 3,000 men in Syria. The U.S.S.R. has approximately 4,000 in Syria and her pilots are manning the later verion MIGs.
COMBAT EFFECTIVENESS
   Excellent

TAIWAN

Defense Budget	$ 750,000,000
Population	15,315,000
Manpower in the Armed Forces	490,000
Defense as % of GNP	9.5%

ARMY

MANPOWER
    340,000 men (Reserves of 1-million)
GENERAL
    Organized into 20 divisions: 2 armored, 12 infantry, 6 light, plus 4 special forces groups, 3 armored cavalry regiments, 2 airborne brigades.
PRINCIPAL EQUIPMENT
    Weapons: 500+ M-24/41 Tanks
                200 M-18 Tank Destroyers
                 80 M-47/48 Tanks
                200+ Armored Personnel Carriers
                1200+ Artillery Pieces
    Missiles: Nike Hercules
                Hawk
    Aircraft: 50 UH-1 Helicopters
                  6 H-34 Helicopters
                  2 KH-4 Helicopters

NAVY

MANPOWER
    35,000 men (Reserves of 60,000)
PRINCIPAL EQUIPMENT
    Vessels: 2 Submarines
                18 Destroyer Escorts
                10 Destroyers
                 6 Torpedo Boats
                15 Coastal Minesweepers
                 2 Inshore Minesweepers
                 1 Minelayer
                21 Tank Landing Craft
                 1 Landing Ship
                15 Medium Landing Ships
                 5 Large Landing Ships
                 1 Escort Transport
                 9 Sub Chasers

Marine Forces:
    2 Divisions with 35,000 men.

AIR FORCE

MANPOWER
    80,000 men (Reserves of 130,000)

PRINCIPAL EQUIPMENT
    Aircraft:
	Fighter-Bombers	90 F-100s
		75 F-5s
	Interceptors	60 F-104s
	Reconnaissance	8 RF-104s
	Transports	40 C-46s
		25 C-47s
		35 C-119s
		10 C-123s
	ASW Patrol	10 S-2s
	Helicopters	10 UH-1s
		10 UH-16s

    <u>Missiles</u>:   Sidewinder

BASES
    Taipei, Hsinchu, Chiai, T'ai-an, Tao-yuan, T'ai-chung, Ping-tung, Kung-K'uang.

MISCELLANEOUS DATA

DEFENSE AGREEMENTS
    U.S.
MAP TYPE ASSISTANCE RECEIVED FROM
    U.S.
INTERNAL SECURITY FORCES
    175,000 men
CONSCRIPTION LAW
    Conscription for 2 years with follow-on reserve obligation.
NATIONAL FLAG
    A red field with a blue rectangle in the upper left corner containing a 12-pointed white sun.
OFFICIAL LANGUAGE
    Mandarin Chinese
COMBAT EFFECTIVENESS
    Excellent

TANZANIA

Defense Budget	$ 41,000,000
Population	15,509,000
Manpower in the Armed Forces	15,000
Defense as % of GNP	3.0%

ARMY

MANPOWER
   13,000 men

GENERAL
   Organized into 4 infantry, 1 artillery battalions, and 1 tank company.

PRINCIPAL EQUIPMENT
   Weapons: Conventional
             20 T-69 Tanks
             16 T-59 Tanks
             14 T-62 Tanks
             15 BTR-152 Armored Personnel Carriers
             Scout Cars
             Light Artillery

NAVY

MANPOWER
   600 men

PRINCIPAL EQUIPMENT
   Vessels: 6 Patrol Boats

AIR FORCE

MANPOWER
   1,000 men

PRINCIPAL EQUIPMENT
   Aircraft: Fighters   15 MIG-17s
                              12 MIG-19s
               Transports   1 An-2
                               3 DH Beavers
                              10 DH Caribous
                               1 HS 748
               Helicopters   2 Bell 206s
                               2 Bell 47s

BASES
   Dar es Salaam, Tabora, Zanzibar, Mbeya, Arusha, Mikumi.

MISCELLANEOUS DATA

DEFENSE AGREEMENTS
   U.A.R.

MAP TYPE ASSISTANCE RECEIVED FROM
   Red China, U.K., Canada, Israel, W. Germany, Netherlands, Indonesia, E. Germany.

INTERNAL SECURITY FORCES
   8,500 men
CONSCRIPTION LAW
   Compulsory for 2 years.
NATIONAL FLAG
   A green triangle in the upper left and a blue one in the lower right, separated by a black band bordered on both sides by yellow stripes.
OFFICIAL LANGUAGE
   English and Swahili
COMBAT EFFECTIVENESS
   Limited
SPECIAL NOTES
   Tanzania has accepted substantial aid from Red China. The Chinese have made excellent progress on a railroad which will run between Zambia to transport its copper to coastal ports.

THAILAND

Defense Budget	$ 750,000,000
Population	38,000,000
Manpower in the Armed Forces	195,000
Defense as % of GNP	4.7%

DEFENSE ESTABLISHMENT

The King is commander-in-chief of the armed forces. The Minister of Defense is charged with the supervision and administration of the Army, Navy and Air Force.

Each service is headed by a commander-in-chief, who functions similarly to those in U.S. service.

ARMY

MANPOWER
   130,000 men (Reserves of 200,000)
GENERAL
   Organized into regional Army commands for tactical and administrative purposes. Each Army area is divided into military circles which are subdivided into military districts.
   There are four infantry divisions (including 3 tank battalions), two independent regimental combat teams.
PRINCIPAL EQUIPMENT
   Weapons: Est. 200 M-24/41 Tanks
                 200+ Armored Personnel Carriers
                 Over 150 Artillery Pieces over 105mm
                 Light Artillery
   Aircraft: 16 Hiller OH-13s Helicopters
                 3 Jet Rangers
                 6 Hiller OH-23s
                 4 CH-47s
                 77 UH-1Hs
   Missiles: Hawk

NAVY

MANPOWER
   23,500 men (of which 9,000 are Marines)
GENERAL
   Three operational groups: Royal Fleet, Royal Marines and the Naval District.
PRINCIPAL EQUIPMENT
   Vessels: 8 Frigates
                14 Patrol Vessels
                 1 Escort Minesweeper
                 4 Coastal Minesweepers
                 2 Coastal Minelayers
                24 Gunboats
                38 Patrol Boats
                 7 Landing Ships
                 8 Landing Craft

Aircraft: 10 S-2F Trackers
            3 C-47s
            2 HU-16Bs
Missiles: Seacat

AIR FORCE

MANPOWER
   30,000 men

GENERAL
   Composed of four groups: Combat, Logistics, Training and Special Services.

PRINCIPAL EQUIPMENT
   Aircraft: Fighter-Bombers   12 F-5s
                                  30 A-4Bs
               Fighter-Recon   2 RT-33s
                                   4 RF-5s
               Counter-
                 insurgency   32 OV-10s
                                  20 AT-6s
                                  45 T-28s
                                  13 AU-23s
               Helicopters   50 UH-1Hs
                                   4 CH-47s
                                  12 Bell KH-4s
                                  19 UH-19s
                                  20 CH-34s
                                   3 HH-43s
               Transports   25 C-47s
                                   2 C-54s
                                   5 C-45s
                                  13 C-123s
   Missiles: Sidewinder

BASES
   Don Muang, Udorn, Ubon, Chieng Mai, Lop Buri, Takli, Prachuab, Khonkaen, Sattahip, U-Tapap, Nakhon Phanom.

MISCELLANEOUS DATA

DEFENSE AGREEMENTS
   U.S.

MAP TYPE ASSISTANCE RECEIVED FROM
   U.S.

INTERNAL SECURITY FORCES
   Border Police - 14,000 with about 50 helicopters. Volunteer Defense Corps - 50,000.

CONSCRIPTION LAW
   2 years' minimum service required, 23 years in reserve components.

MILITARY SCHOOLS
   Military Preparatory School, National Defense College, Armed Forces Staff College, Royal Military Academy, Royal Naval Academy, Royal Air Force Academy, SEATO Technical Schools, Naval Officers College, Flying Training School, Air Command & General Staff College, Army War College.

THAILAND

NATIONAL FLAG
   Horizontal stripes of red, white, blue (double width), white, red.
OFFICIAL LANGUAGE
   Thai
COMBAT EFFECTIVENESS
   Limited. Thais would require outside support for any prolonged military operations.
SPECIAL NOTES
   The role of the military has been de-emphasized by the present government which appears to want to direct its energies towards social and economic needs.
   Insurgent activity in northeast alone is estimated to involve 8,500 men under arms.

Defense Budget	$ 6,000,000
Population	2,000,000
Manpower intthe Armed Forces	1,500
Defense as % of GNP	2.3%

ARMY

MANPOWER
 1,500 men

GENERAL
 Organized into 1 infantry battalion, 1 reconnaissance unit, 1 engineer unit, and support units.

PRINCIPAL EQUIPMENT
<u>Weapons</u>: 5 Armored Cars
 Conventional Arms
<u>Aircraft</u>: 1 C-47 Transport
 2 Broussard Liaison
 1 Alouette Helicopter
<u>Vessels</u>: 3 Patrol Boats
 1 River Gunboat

NAVY

None.

AIR FORCE

None.
 Army operates as only service.

MISCELLANEOUS DATA

DEFENSE AGREEMENTS
 Union Africane et Malgache

MAP TYPE ASSISTANCE RECEIVED FROM
 Israel, France, U.S., U.S.S.R.

INTERNAL SECURITY FORCES
 1,300 men

CONSCRIPTION LAW
 Volunteer forces

NATIONAL FLAG
 5 alternating horizontal stripes of green and yellow, with a white star in the upper left corner centered in a red square.

OFFICIAL LANGUAGE
 French

SPECIAL NOTES
 Military took control of government in 1967 and has continued in control since that time.

TRINIDAD & TOBAGO

Defense Budget $ 4,000,000
Population 1,200,000
Manpower in the Armed Forces 1,100
Defense as % of GNP 0.6%

ARMY

MANPOWER
　　1,000 men (Reserves of 1,000)
GENERAL
　　Organized into 1 infantry battalion and support units.
PRINCIPAL EQUIPMENT
　　Weapons:　Conventional
　　　　　　　Armored Cars
　　　　　　　2 Light Aircraft
　　　　　　　2 Helicopters

COAST GUARD

MANPOWER
　　100 men
PRINCIPAL EQUIPMENT
　　Vessels:　2 Patrol Gunboats
　　　　　　　2 Patrol Craft

AIR FORCE

　　None.

MISCELLANEOUS DATA

MAP TYPE ASSISTANCE RECEIVED FROM
　　U.S., U.K.
INTERNAL SECURITY FORCES
　　250 men
CONSCRIPTION LAW
　　Volunteer forces
NATIONAL FLAG
　　Red with a black diagonal stripe bordered in white.
OFFICIAL LANGUAGE
　　English
COMBAT EFFECTIVENESS
　　Negligible

Defense Budget	$ 45,000,000
Population	5,800,000
Manpower in the Armed Forces	24,000
Defense as % of GNP	4.5%

DEFENSE ESTABLISHMENT

The President is Commander-in-Chief of the armed forces. There is a Secretariat of State for National Defense, directly attached to the Presidency of the Council. A chief of the general staff at the top of the military hierarchy is responsible for command.

ARMY

MANPOWER
    20,000 men
GENERAL
    The mission of the Army is three-fold: to defend the country's territorial integrity; to maintain internal security; and, to participate in military civic action.
    Organized into 1 armored, 5 infantry, 1 commando, 1 artillery and 1 engineer battalion.
PRINCIPAL EQUIPMENT
    Weapons: Light Weapons
               Light and Heavy Artillery
               30 AMX-13 Tanks
               20 M-41 Tanks
               60 Armored Cars

NAVY

MANPOWER
    2,000 men
GENERAL
    Coast Guard type duties only.
PRINCIPAL EQUIPMENT
    Vessels: 1 Escort
               1 Corvette
               3 Patrol Boats (with SS-12 SSM)
               1 Patrol Vessel
               11 Coastal Patrol Boats

AIR FORCE

MANPOWER
    2,000 men
GENERAL
    Air Force is responsible for: preserving the integrity of the national borders, assisting the Army, National Guard in internal security, and air-sea rescue operations.

TUNISIA

PRINCIPAL EQUIPMENT
    Aircraft: 12 F-86s
                   12 SAAB-91D Safir
                    8 Aeromacchi MB 326s
                    3 Flamant Light Transports
                    8 Alouette II/III Helicopters

BASES
    Bizerte, Djerba-Melita, Gafsa, Sfax-El-Maou.

MISCELLANEOUS DATA

DEFENSE AGREEMENTS
    Arab League

MAP TYPE ASSISTANCE RECEIVED FROM
    Turkey, W. Germany, France, Italy, Sweden, UAR, U.K., U.S.

INTERNAL SECURITY FORCES
    5,000 Gendarmerie, 4,500 National Guard

CONSCRIPTION LAW
    Compulsory for one year

MILITARY SCHOOLS
    Military Academy

NATIONAL FLAG
    A red field with a white disc containing a red crescent and star.

OFFICIAL LANGUAGE
    Arabic

COMBAT EFFECTIVENESS
    Limited

TURKEY

Defense Budget	$ 1,000,000,000
Population	40,850,000
Manpower in the Armed Forces	450,000
Defense as % of GNP	4.2%

ARMY

MANPOWER
  375,000 men (Reserves of 800,000)
GENERAL
  Organized into 6 army corps; 1 armored division, 2 mechanized infantry divisions, 12 infantry divisions, 4 armored cavalry brigades, 4 armored brigades, 3 mechanized infantry battalions, 2 parachute battalions, 3 missile battalions.
PRINCIPAL EQUIPMENT
  Weapons: 1,800+ M-47/48 Tanks
                     M-24/41 Tanks
                     M-36 TanksDestroyers
                     M-8 Armored Cars
             500+ M-59/113 Armored Personnel Carriers
             Light and Heavy Artillery
  Aircraft: 15 Do-27 Transports
             18 Cessna U-17s
             9 Do-28 Transports
             5 Beech Barons
             20 Bell 206s
             20 Bell 47s
  Missiles: SS-11 AT
             Cobra AT
             Honest John

NAVY

MANPOWER
  36,500 men (Reserves of 70,000)
PRINCIPAL EQUIPMENT
  Vessels: 15 Submarines
             14 Destroyers
             6 Sub Chasers
             7 Escort Vessels
             15 Escort/Minesweepers
             4 Inshore Minesweepers
             8 Minelayers
             90 Landing Craft
             14 Motor Launches
             20 Motor Gunboats
             11 Torpedo Boats
             40 Auxiliaries
             1 Training Ship
             1 Sub Rescue Ship
  Aircraft: 12 S-2 Tracker ASW
             3 AB-205 ASW Helicopters

TURKEY   217

AIR FORCE

MANPOWER
    50,000 men (Reserves of 80,000)
PRINCIPAL EQUIPMENT
    Aircraft: Fighter-Bombers   20 F-4s
                                  25 F-5s
                                  32 F-104s
                                  60 F-100s
                Interceptors   32 F-5s
                Reconnaissance   24 RF-84s
                                  12 RF-5s
                Transports   14 C-47s
                                  10 C-130s
                                  36 Transalls
                Helicopters   10 Bell UH-1s
                                  10 Sikorsky UH-19s
                                   4 Bell 204s
    Missiles: Nike-Ajac
                Nike-Hercules
                Sidewinder
                Bullpup
BASES
    Diyarbakir, Esenboga, Cigli, Bandirma, Graziemir, Balikesir, Merzifon, Eskisehir, Yesilkoy, Sivas, Etimesgut, Murted, Konya.

MISCELLANEOUS DATA

DEFENSE AGREEMENTS
    NATO, CENTO
MAP TYPE ASSISTANCE RECEIVED FROM
    U.S., U.K.
INTERNAL SECURITY FORCES
    95,000 men
CONSCRIPTION LAW
    20 months' compulsory service for all males.
NATIONAL FLAG
    A white star and crescent on a red field.
OFFICIAL LANGUAGE
    Turkish
COMBAT EFFECTIVENESS
    Excellent
SPECIAL NOTES
    Since the Cyprus invasion in 1975, relations between U.S. and Turkey have been strained and government took control of most U.S. bases in country.

Defense Budget	$ 52,000,000
Population	11,683,000
Manpower in the Armed Forces	21,000
Defense as % of GNP	5.1%

ARMY

MANPOWER
    20,000 men

GENERAL
    Organized into 6 infantry battalions, 1 mechanized battalion, 2 parachute/commando battalions, 1 battalion of border guards, 1 artillery regiment.

PRINCIPAL EQUIPMENT
    Weapons: Conventional
                58 T-54/55 Tanks
                15 Ferret Scout Cars
                12 M-4 Tanks
                60 BTR-40/152 Armored Personnel Carriers
                12 OT-64 Armored Personnel Carriers
                Light Artillery
    Missiles: Guideline
                Scud

NAVY

None.

AIR FORCE

MANPOWER
    1,000 men

PRINCIPAL EQUIPMENT
    Aircraft: Fighter-Bombers   15 MIG-15s
                                        14 MIG-17s
                Counter-
                  Insurgency   10 Magisters
                Transports   3 C-47s
                                        1 DH Caribou
                Helicopters   7 Mi-4s
                                        5 Bell 206s
                                        5 Bell 205s

MISCELLANEOUS DATA

MAP TYPE ASSISTANCE RECEIVED FROM
    Czechoslovakia, India, Israel, Pakistan, U.S., U.S.S.R.

INTERNAL SECURITY FORCES
    1,000 men

CONSCRIPTION LAW
    Volunteer forces

UGANDA

NATIONAL FLAG
Six alternate horizontal stripes of black, yellow and red, with a crested crane on a white circle in the center.
OFFICIAL LANGUAGE
English
COMBAT EFFECTIVENESS
Limited
SPECIAL NOTES
Uganda President Amin suspended civil rule and invoked martial law and assumed all powers. As chairman of the OAU, he has called for the invasion of Rhodesia and South Africa.

Defense Budget	$ 95,800,000,000*
Population	250,000,000
Manpower in the Armed Forces	3,375,000
Defense as % of GNP	Est. 9%

DEFENSE ESTABLISHMENT

Overall direction of the Armed Forces is vested in the Ministry of Defense. They comprise five services: the Strategic Rocket Forces, the Air Defense Forces, the Ground Forces, the Air Force, and the Navy. Each service has its fighting arms.

GROUND FORCES

MANPOWER
   2,000,000 men

GENERAL
   The Ground Forces (Army) are organized into 165 divisions: 108 motorized infantry, 50 tank, 7 airborn divisions, of which, about 125 are 75% strength.
   There are 20 divisions in East Germany; 2 in Poland; 4 in Hungary; 5 in Czechoslovakia; 45 are in the Soviet Far East; 61 in European USSR; 5 in Central USSR; 23 in Southern USSR.

PRINCIPAL EQUIPMENT
   The Ground Forces possess tactical missiles; new tanks; armored troop carriers; conventional and rocket artillery; anti-tank weapons; self-propelled anti-aircraft, missile and artillery mounts; Their main fire-power is made up of tactical nuclear rockets. The motorized infantry divisions have 12,000 men and 265 tanks, with a tremendous number of armored personnel carriers. Airborne divisions have 7,000 men and 45 SP guns. Armored (Tank) divisions have 9,500 men and 564 tanks. There are 108 motorized infantry, 7 airborne and 50 tank divisions.
   The Soviet Ground Forces are estimated to have 38,000 tanks (7,500 in East Germany, 1,128 in Hungary, 1,130 in Poland, and 2,820 in Czechoslovakia).
   It is estimated that the Warsaw Pact countries have about 19,000 tanks in Central Europe. Some 20,400 T-62s and 24,300 T-55s have been produced since 1968. The Soviet armed forces have over 300,000 military vehicles. Soviet tank production capability exists to produce 460 tanks per month.
   Soviet Ground Forces use massive quantities of artillery (primarily 100/122/130/152/203mm) with about 25% of manpower artillerymen.

* See Special Notes.

U.S.S.R.

```
        Rocket Launchers:      122/140mm
        Anti-Tank Weapons:     85mm, 100mm, 57mm
        Tactical Missiles:     Sagger, Snapper, Swatter
        Surface-to-Surface
           Missiles:           Frog, Scud, Scaleboard
                               Est. over 1,000 Launchers
        Surface-to-Air
           Missiles:           SA-2,4,6,7s
```

NAVAL FORCES

MANPOWER
    500,000 men

GENERAL
    The Soviet Navy operates with four large naval commands: Baltic, Northern, Pacific and Black Sea fleets. It is believed that the operational submarine command is directly attached to the Senior Military Council.
    The Naval Forces consist of: the submarine branch, the surface fleet, the marine light infantry and naval aviation.

PRINCIPAL EQUIPMENT

```
    Submarine Fleet:    70 SLBMs (50 nuclear/20 diesel)
                        30 Attack (nuclear)
                        40 Cruise Missile (nuclear)
                       140 Attack (diesel)
                        25 Cruise Missile (diesel)
                        10 Coastal (diesel)
```

The Submarine Branch is considered the main component of the naval forces, comprises 315 units. Of these, 120 are nuclear powered and the Soviets are phasing-out diesels rapidly. They are producing nuclear powered submarines at a rate of 15 to 16 annually. If present obsolescence patterns hold, they will have fewer attack and cruise missile units in the fleet toward the early 1980's; however, the newer units have far greater capabilities.

```
    Surface Fleet:        2 ASW Helicopter Carriers
                         30 Cruisers (most with SSM/SAM)
                         42 Destroyers (missile)
                         36 Destroyers (conventional)
                        118 Escorts
                        150 Submarine Chasers
                        151 Missile Patrol Boats
                        225 Motor Torpedo Boats
                        230 Landing Craft
                        195 Minesweepers
                         25 Hydrofoils
                        200+ Service Vessels
                       1300+ Auxiliaries
```

The surface fleet has had a reduction in the number of units over past years. However, the newer units all substantially increased performance in range and firepower.

The Marine Light Infantry's mission is to carry out diversionary operations of a commando-type nature and assist in coastal defense. The strength is estimated to be 15,000 men.

Coastal Defense comprises an observation and communications service, fixed and mobile coastal artillery units, and anti-aircraft artillery service and the interceptor fighter aircraft of the Navy's aviation branch. Apart from the coastal areas, the navy has a responsibility for protecting the coastline to an inland distance of 50 miles.

<u>Naval Aviation (land-based)</u>:

```
         60    Tu-22 Strike-Recon
         50    Tu-95 NATO Recon
         40    Il-28 Torpedo Bombers
        140    Il-18 ASW
        275    Tu-16 Anti-shipping
                  w/missiles
        130    Tu-16 Recon & Aerial Tankers
         80    Il-28 ASW
         95    Be-2 ASW
        240    Mi-4 & Ka-25 Helicopters
         80    Be-12 ASW Amphibians
       200+    Transports
```

<u>Missiles</u>:

```
    Kelt      Kipper
    Styx      Goa
    Serb      Sawfly
    Guide     Shaddock
    Ganef     Giffon
    Galosh    Gainful
    Sark      Scrubber
    Styx
```

Soviet nuclear submaries have a total of 720 intercontinental range ballistic missiles in service.

The Soviet Navy has launched its first aircraft carrier, which is believed to be in the 30/40,000 ton class (Kiev) similar to our Hancock class. It is about 600 feet long and will use VTOL aircraft inasmuch as no deck catapults have been observed. A second such vessel has been reported as under construction.

<u>AIR DEFENSE FORCES</u>

MANPOWER
    500,000 men
GENERAL
    These comprise surface-to-air missile troops, missile-carrying aircraft, radar and special troops.

U.S.S.R.

PRINCIPAL EQUIPMENT
    Aircraft: Over 3200 Fighter-Interceptors
                   700 MIG-17/19/21s
                   200 Yak-25s
                   800 Su-9s
                 1100 Yak-28s
                   150 Tu-28s
                   600 Su-11/15s
                 200+ MIG-25s
                    20 Tu-144 AEW Aircraft
    Surface-to-Air Missiles:
        Guideline
        Goa
        Ganef
        Gainful
        Griffon

        Est. Over 10,000 launchers with 15 per site.

    Anti-Ballistic Missiles:
        Galosh

        Est. 50 deployed on outskirts of Moskow.

The territory of the USSR is divided into air defense regions - Moscow and Baku as headquarters locations. In the coastal areas, the use of interception and naval air units is controlled by Air Defense Forces.
Anti-aircraft artillery throughout Soviet Union is under control of Air Defense Command. Outside the USSR, this control extends to air defense systems in East Germany, Poland and Hungary.

STRATEGIC ROCKET FORCES

MANPOWER
    350,000 men
GENERAL
    SRF constitute the key Soviet strike force and this Command exercises control over: ICBM's (both ground based and those in submarines) plus, the strategic bomber force.
PRINCIPAL EQUIPMENT
    Intercontinental Ballistic Missiles
    Total: 1,576
       190 SS-7
        20 SS-8
       288 SS-9
     1018 SS-11
        60 SS-13

Intermediate Range Ballistic Missiles and Medium Range Ballistic Missiles (mobile)

Total: 660
- 100 SS-5 (IRBM)
- 500 SS-4 (MMRBM)

Submarine Launched Intercontinental Ballistic Missiles

Total: 720
- SS-N-4/6/6/8s

AIR FORCE

MANPOWER

500,000 men (Reserves of 3-million)

GENERAL

The Soviet Air Force is divided into three branches: Long-Range Aviation, Frontal Air Armies (Tactical) and Air Transport Command. Both Air Defense and Navy have control of own air arms.

Long-Range Aviation

Total: 160
- 50 TU-95 Bears (nuclear weapons)
- 90 Mya-4 Bisons (nuclear weapons)
- 50 Mya-4 Bisons (aerial tankers)
- 20 Tupelov Backfire (nuclear weapons)

Frontal Air Armies (Tactical)

Total: Over 4,000 Aircraft
- 170 Yak-28
- 800+ MIG-17
- 600+ Su-7s
- 500+ MIG-23
- 1500 MIG-21
- Il-28
- Su-20

Transport Command

Total: Over 1,700 Aircraft
- 750 An-12
- 40 An-22
- 1000+ Il-14, An-8/24s
- 50 Il-18
- Over 3,000 Helicopters (Mi-1/2/4/6/8/10/12/24s)
- (2000+ aircraft of Aeroflot (Soviet Airline) available as civil reserve fleet.)

U.S.S.R.   225

MISCELLANEOUS DATA

MILITARY SCHOOLS

Colleges (4-year)

Military Education	- Moscow
Military Political	- Moscow
Military Political	- Novosibirsk
Military Political	- Lemberg
Armor/Artillery	- Sverdlovsk
Engineers	- Simferopol
Air Force	- Kurgan
Tech. & Transp.	- Donetsk
Air Defense	- Lenigrad
Navy	- Kiev
Rostov Military	- Rostov

General Military Colleges (4-year)

Alma Ata, Baku, Kiev, Leningrad, Moscow, Omsk, Ordzhonikidze and Tashkent.
Far Eastern Military - Blagoveshchensk

Engineer Military Colleges (4-year)

Kazan, Perm, Rostov, Saratov, Serpukhov, Charkov and Riga.

Armor Colleges (4-year)

Blagoveshchensk, S amark, Kazan, Chirchik (Uzbekistan), Ulyanovsk, Charkov and Chelyabisnk.

Armored Maintenance (4-year)

Kiev and Minsk

Air Defense (4-year)

Armavir (Armenia), Stavropol, Schitomir, Leningrad, Engels and Yaroslavi.

Artillery (4-year)

Kiev, Orenburg, Poltava, Leningrad, Smolensk.

Aircraft and Missile Engineering (1-year)

Minsk

Radio-Tech. - Engineers (5-year)

Kiev

Air Defense Middle Schools (3-year)

Vilna, Gorki, Daugavpils (Lettland), Krasnoyarsk, Opochka (Pskov area) and Ordzhonikidze.

Air Force (4-year)
Volograd, Eistk (Krasnodor, Chernigov, Borisoglebsk (Voronezh), Tambov, Orenburg, Barnaul (Altai), Balashov (Saratov), Syzran (Kubiyshev), Voroshilovgrad and Chelyabinsk.

Air Force Middle Schools (3-year)
Saratov, Tambov, Voronezh, Kaliningrad, Vasilkov, Charkov (2), Perm, Atschinsk and Irkutsk.

Navy Colleges (5-year)
Leningrad, Vladivostok, Baku, Kaliningrad, Sevastopol.

Engineering (4-year)
Kaliningrad, Tuymen and Kamenez-Podolsk.

Technical (4-year)
Ulyanovsk

Engineer-Technical (5-year)
Leningrad

Artillery Colleges (4-year)
Kolomna, Leningrad, Odessa, Sumy, Tbilisi, Tula and Khmeinitski.

Middle School for Artillery (3-year)
Tambov

Transportation Colleges (4-year)
Gorki, Kemerovo, Novotscherask, Potlava, Ryazan, Tomsk, Ulyanovsk, Cherepovets, Kiev and Stavropol.

Chemical (4-year)
Kostroma and Saratov

Vehicle Maintenance (4-year)
Ryazan, Ussurisk, Chelyabinsk.

Civil Defense (3-year)
Balashikha

Backland Service (4-year)
Volsk

U.S.S.R.   227

>   **Railroad & Traffic (4-year)**
>   Leningrad
>
>   **Military Technicians & Electricians Middle School**
>   Therm
>
>   **Engineer Middle Schools (3-year)**
>   Kamueschin and Leningrad

NATIONAL FLAG
   Red, with sickle and hammer in gold in upper corner near the staff, and above them a 5-pointed star bordered in gold.

OFFICIAL LANGUAGE
   Russian
COMBAT EFFECTIVENESS
   Excellent
SPECIAL NOTES
   Coastal Defense forces come under control of the Navy.
   The Soviet Defense Budget is stated as a "dollar equivalency to U.S. costs". Most Western experts feel that the listed defense budget represents only a fraction of the actual national security expenditure. It does not include such items as procurement of nuclear warheads, R&D for new weapons systems, and the military part of the space program.

   General agreement exists that a substantial part of the Soviet Science Budget is spent for military purposes, for which no breakdown has been shown since 1957. Even at that time, 60% of the 'science' budget could not be accounted for by the breakdown published.
   Additionally, military expenditures can also be hidden in the large unexplained residuals in the overall budget and in the national economy sub-budget and in the unlisted allocations to such ministries as aviation industry, defense industry, electronics industry, and medium machine building.

   Attempts to equate ruble data to dollars is ineffective inasmuch as their pricing system is different from ours in that prices applied to physical resources and labor in one part of the economy may not be the same as in another; the Soviet government can fix such prices for its own accounting purposes as a way of allocating resources and manpower not linked to the market mechanisms of the nation. On average, the Soviets obtain their defense as less cost than the U.S.; for example, due to lower manual labor costs.

A "dollar equivalency" in purchasing power is a more logical approach to gaining an insight into the Soviet Defense Budget.

Because the U.S. defense budget is an open document, one can equate for total manpower per head and cost for 'active' forces and compute it represents 40% of the total budget. Adding to this the National Guard, Reserve, and Civilian employees ads an additional 15%... for total manpower costs of 55% of total budget. The balance is procurement, R&D, etc. The U.S. will have 2,152,000 active forces and 880,366 in National Guard and Reserve, with 1,027,327 civilian employees. For Fy-1975, this 'active' cost is $15,800 or a total of $34-Billion. This would make comparable Soviet costs for 'active' forces $53-Billion. Guard, Reserve and Civilian employees average at $6,750 or $12.9-Billion (total manpower cost $46.9-Billion) for the U.S... Soviet Reserves and Security forces are estimated at $1-Million. Thus, a cost of an additional $6.7-Billion for a total manpower cost of $60-Billion.

Soviet personnel costs have been in the order of 30-35% of their total budget. Authorities suggest that the Soviet Science budget has about 70% covering military R&D which would represent non-manpower costs of an additional 17.9-billion rubles or an additional $35.8-billion. This would bring the Soviet defense total to $95.8-billion or $3.2-billion over the requested Fy-1975 total obligational authority of the U.S. defense budget ($92.6-billion).

The Soviets have four new ICBM's under development: SS-X-16, 17, 18 and 19. They have deployed a new SLBM designated SS-N-8 with a 4,000 n.m. range. They have also deployed two new SLBM submarines, Delta I & II. They have just deployed a new strategic bomber - Code name, "Backfire", with a Mach 2.0 capability.

Under SALT I, the following was agreed to:

	U.S.	U.S.S.R.
ICBM's	1,054	1,530
SLBM's	710	1,016

The Vladivostok meeting resulted in a revised strategic arms agreement that (1) guarantee's there will be no meaningful reduction in nuclear arms at least until 1985, and (2) the USSR is allowed a missile force three times as large as the U.S. one, if measured by the most relevant criterion - 'throw-weight'.

There are Soviet landing fields and naval bases in Somalia on the horn of Africa and in Yemen and a new naval base on the island of Socotra.

A Soviet naval and air base at Um Qasr in Iraq, at the head of the Persian Gulf.

UNITED ARAB EMIRATES

Defense Budget (See Special Note at end)
Population 656,000
Manpower in the Armed Forces 18,500
Defense as % of GNP N.A.

PRELIMINARY COMMENTARY

The United Arab Emirates came into being in 1971, being then joined by the seven Trucial Coast Sheikhdoms of Abu Dhabi, Ajman, Dubai, Fujairah, Sharjah, Umm el Quwain, and Ras al Khaimah.

ARMY

MANPOWER
 15,000 men

GENERAL
 Comprises 6 infantry battalions, 3 armored car regiments, 1 artillery regiment, 2 1/3 missile battalions.

PRINCIPAL EQUIPMENT
 Weapons: Conventional
  100+ Saladin Armored Cars
   25 Ferret Scout Cars
   10 Scorpion and Land Rover AVs
    6 Shortland AVs
 Missiles: 28 Firing Units - Rapier
  Vigilant AT

NAVY

MANPOWER
 500 men

PRINCIPAL EQUIPMENT
 Vessels: 3 Patrol Craft
  6 Patrol Boats
  4 Powered Launches
  2 Dhows

AIR FORCE

MANPOWER
 3,000 men

PRINCIPAL EQUIPMENT
 Aircraft: Strike/TAC Recon 32 Mirage Vs
  Fighter-Bombers 18 Mirage IIIs
    8 Hunters
  Armed Trainers 4 MB-326s
  Transports 16 Short Skyvans
    3 C-130s
    2 BAC VC-10s
  Helicopters 12 Bell 206s

MISCELLANEOUS DATA

DEFENSE AGREEMENTS
    Arab League
MAP TYPE ASSISTANCE RECEIVED FROM
    Pakistan, Britain, Arab League
INTERNAL SECURITY FORCES
    N.A.
CONSCRIPTION LAW
    Volunteer forces (almost all officers foreign mercenaries)
NATIONAL FLAG
    Each state has its own.
OFFICIAL LANGUAGE
    Arabic
COMBAT EFFECTIVENESS
    Limited
SPECIAL NOTES
    Defense budget is undeterminable in light of massive financial aid from Arab League members - $355,000,000 last year for aircraft alone.

UNITED KINGDOM   231

    Defense Budget $ 5,632,000,000
    Population   55,962,000
    Manpower in the Armed Forces   333,600
    Defense as % of GNP   5.5%

ARMY

MANPOWER
    167,500 men (107,200 Regular Reserve and 58,500
    Volunteer Reserves)
GENERAL
    Organized 1 Corps and 4 Divisional headquarters; 14
    armored regiments; 5 armored recon regiments; 26 artil-
    lery regiments; 14 engineer regiments; 50 battalions
    of infantry; 5 Gurkha battalions; 1 special air services
    regiment.
PRINCIPAL EQUIPMENT
    Weapons: 950 Chieftain Tanks
                180 Scorpion Tanks
                100 Centurion Tanks
                Saladin and Ferret Armored Cars
                Saracen Armored Personnel Carriers
                Centurion Mk V Bridgelayer Tanks
                Centurion Mk II Recovery Vehicle
                Light and Heavy Artillery
    Missiles: Honest Jogh
                Lance
                Carl Gustav
                Vigilant AT
                Swingfire AT
                Rapier
                Blowpipe
                Thunderbird
    Aircraft: 200+ Light Aircraft
                300+ Helicopters

NAVY

MANPOWER
    75,600 men (27,700 Regular REserve and 5,800
    Volunteer Reserve)
PRINCIPAL EQUIPMENT
    Vessels: 1 Aircraft Carrier
                 1 ASW Carrier
                23 Submarines
                 1 Assault Ship
                 1 Cruiser
                 9 Guided Missile Destroyers
                33 General Purpose Frigates
                13 ASW Frigates
                37 Minesweepers
                 1 Depot Ship
                 1 MCM Support Ship
                 1 Diving Trials Ship

              1 Trials Ship
              5 Coastal Patrol Ships
              3 Fast Target Boats
              4 Fast Patrol Boats
              2 Seaward Defense Vessels
              1 Hospital Ship
             13 Survey Vessels
              1 Submarine Tenter
              4 Offshore Patrol Boats
              2 Patrol Craft
              4 Ba-listic Missile Submarines (Polaris
                 Missiles)
              9 Nuclear Submarines
              2 Hovercraft
   Aircraft: Strike   12 Buccaneer S2s
              Air Defense   16 Phantom FGls
                                  24 Gannet AEW.3s
              Helicopters   72 Sea Kings
                                  80 Wasps
                                 140 Wessex
                                  30 Gazelles
                                 100 Westland W.13s
   Missiles: Sea Wolf
              Sea Skua
              Sea Dart
              Sidewinder
              Sparrow
              Bullpup
              Sea Slug
              Seacat
              Martel
              Exocet
              Ikara
BASES, AIR
    Culdrose, Lee-on-Solent, Portland, Yeovilton,
    Prestwick.

AIR FORCE

MANPOWER
    90,500 men (31,900 Regular Reserve and 200 Volunteer
    Reserve)
PRINCIPAL EQUIPMENT
   Aircraft: Strike   72 Vulcan B2s
                                   50 Buccaneers
                                   40 Jaguars
              Air Defense   80 Lightning
                                   20 F4s
              Reconnaissance   24 Canberras
                                   12 Vulcans
                                   40 RF4s
              Offensive Support   80 Harriers
                                   40 Jaguars
              AEW   20 Shackletons

UNITED KINGDOM 233

	Maritime Patrol	40 Nimrods
	Strategic Trans-Transports	14 Belfasts
		14 VC-10s
	Tactical-Transports	64 C-130s
	Support Helicopters	60 Wessex
		40 Pumas
	Tankers	24 Victors
	Search and Rescue	35 Wessex
		12 Whirlwinds

Missiles: Bloodhound
Rapier
Firestreak
Red Top
Tigercat
Sparrow
Sidewinder
Martel
SS-11
Advanced Sparrow

BASES
    Over 70 operational with six used by USAAF.

MISCELLANEOUS DATA

DEFENSE AGREEMENTS
    NATO, CENTO, Malaysia, Singapore, Australia, New Zealand, member nations in the Commonwealth.
INTERNAL SECURITY FORCES
    25,000 men
CONSCRIPTION LAW
    Volunteer forces
NATIONAL FLAG
    Superimposition of the red cross of St. Andrew of Scotland, and the red cross of St. Patrick of Ireland, all on a blue background.
OFFICIAL LANGUAGE
    English
COMBAT EFFECTIVENESS
    Excellent
SPECIAL NOTES
    The Royal Navy operates four submarines with 64 Polaris missiles.
    Because of economic problems, Britain is anticipated to incur slight reduction in defense budget over next 5 years.
    Overseas Units stationed in: Berlin (3,000); Hong Kong (9,000); Mediterranean (Cyprus, Malta, Gibraltar) (4,300); W. Germany (55,000); Other areas (600).

Defense Budget			$ 104,000,000,000		
Population			203,212,000		
Manpower in the Armed Forces			2,100,000		
Defense as % of GNP			6.7%		

ARMY

MANPOWER
   785,000 men

GENERAL
   Organized into 13 divisions, but being increased to total of 16:

	Infantry	Mechanized Infantry	Armored	Air Mobile	Airborne
Men	16,531	15,963,	16,259	18,207	14,994
Tanks	85	190	365	0	0
Artillery	76	76	76	54	54
Helicopters	97	97	97	428	97
Fixed-Wing A/C	4	4	6	6	6
Weapons	19,233	20,000	12,000	12,000	9,000
Vehicles	5,000	7,000	5,000	4,000	3,900
No. of Divisions	5	5	4	1	1

Principal Weapons
  8,305 Tanks
  22,000 Armored Personnel Carriers
  2,500 Fixed-Wing Aircraft
  7,000 Helicopters
  6,000 Artillery Pieces
  3,000 Heavy Mortars

Missiles
  Hawk
  Chapparal
  Lance
  SAM D
  Nike Hercules
  Roland
  Stinger
  Redeye

Anti-Tank
TOW
Dragon

Army Reserve Forces
   Army National Guard   379,144
   Army Reserve   232,591

NAVY

MANPOWER
   529,000 men

GENERAL
   Organized into four fleets:
            1st - Eastern Pacific
            2nd - Atlantic
            6th - Mediterranean
            7th - Pacific

Summary of Major Forces
    Commissioned ships in active fleet - 491
    Surface combatants and submarines - 291
    Other vessels - 200

PRINCIPAL EQUIPMENT
    Vessels:
- 13 Aircraft Carriers
- 41 Polaris Submarines with 656 SLBMs
- 73 Attack Submarines
- 7 Cruisers
- 30 Frigates
- 61 Destroyers
- 54 Escorts
- 16 Patrol Vessels
- 9 Mine Warfare Ships
- 65 Amphibious Warfare Ships
- 200 Support Vessels

Carrier Air Groups - 23
Active Aircraft - 1,448
- 312 Fighters (F-4, F-8s, F-14)
- 366 Light Attack (A-4, A-7, A-6, A-4)
- 132 Medium Attack
- 48 Tankers (KA-3s)
- 40 Reconnaissance (RF-8, RF-4s)
- 32 ECM (E6A, EA-3B, EC-130)
- 48 Early Warning (E2B, E1B)
- 311 ASW Fixed-Wing (S-2, S-3A, P-3, P-3s)
- 96 ASW Helicopters (SH-2D, SH-3s)
- 63 Transports

Missiles:
Polaris SLBM	Sea Sparrow
Poseidon SLBM	Subroc
Asroc	SM-2 MR
Standard	Harpoon
Talos	Walleye
Terrier	Shrike

Naval Reserve Forces
    Naval Reserve - 119,231 men

MARINE CORPS

MANPOWER
    196,000 men

GENERAL
    Organized into 3 Divisions, 3 Marine Air Wings.

PRINCIPAL EQUIPMENT
    Weapons:
        700+ Tanks, M-48, M-103, M-60s
        M-113 and LVTP-5 Armored Personnel Carriers
        Light and Heavy Artillery
        Hawk Missiles

Aircraft: 144 F-4 Fighters
            120 A-4 and A-6 Attack
             36 AV-8 Harrier
             36 RF-4 Reconnaissance
             23 EA-6s Reconnaissance
             36 OV-10 and AH-1J Observation
             46 KC-130 Tankers
             70 CH-53D Helicopters
            100 CH-46A Helicopters

Marine Corps Reserve Forces
    Marine Corps Reserve   -   50,000 men

AIR FORCE

MANPOWER
    590,000 men
GENERAL
    Organized into commands: Strategic Air, Tactical Air, Airlift, Training.
PRINCIPAL EQUIPMENT
        Strategic Missiles
         450 Minuteman IIs
         550 Minuteman IIIs
          54 Titan IIs
        1054 Total

   Strategic Bomber Force
     66 F-111s
    180 B-52Gs
     75 B-52Hs
    120 B-52Ds
    615 KC-135 Tankers
     10 SR-71A Reconnaissance
   Total USAF Aircraft Inventory - 7,319 Aircraft

Bombers (B-52, F111, B-57s)	499
Tankers (KC-135)	660
Fighters/Interceptors (F-4, F-101, F-102, F-15, F-104, F-105, F-100, F-111, F-16)	1985
Attack (A-7, A-37, A-10)	323
Reconnaissance (RF-4, RF-101, RB-57, SR-71)	591
Transport (C-121, C-5, C-130, C-123, C-133, C-124, C-135, C-141)	937
Rescue	44
Helicopters	297
Trainers	1896
Others	87

U.S.   237

USAF Reserve Forces
    Air National Guard - 92,291 men
    Air Force Reserve - 49,773 men
                                   142,064 men

U.S. Forces Deployed Overseas

Pacific		Latin America	
Korea	42,000	Panama Canal	9,000
Phillippines	14,000	Puerto Rico	4,000
Taiwan	3,000	Guantanamo	2,000
Japan	48,000	Other	1,000
Guam	10,000		
Seventh Fleet	28,000		
Okinawa	52,500		
Other		**Europe**	
Antartica	3,000	W. Germany	220,000
Morocco	1,000	Britain	21,000
Iran	1,000	Spain	9,000
Ethiopia	1,600	Italy	11,000
Canada, Green-		Netherlands	2,000
land, Iceland	3,000	Greece	2,000
Other	5,000	Belgium	2,000
		Sixth Fleet	30,000

MISCELLANEOUS DATA

DEFENSE AGREEMENTS
    NATO, Rio Pact, Australia, Japan, S. Korea, Taiwan, Phillippines, New Zealand, Turkey, Iran, Pakistan.
INTERNAL SECURITY FORCES
    No national force
CONSCRIPTION LAW
    Volunteer forces
NATIONAL FLAG
    Consisting of 13 horizontal, alternate red and white stripes, and a union of 50 five-pointed stars arranged in alternate rows of 6 and 5 on a blue field in the upper left corner.
OFFICIAL LANGUAGE
    English
MILITARY SCHOOLS
    U.S. Military Academy
    U.S. Naval Academy
    U.S. Air Force Academy
    Command and General Staff College
    Industrial War College
    Naval War College
    Naval Post-Graduate School
    Armed Forces Staff College
    Adjutant Generals School
    Finance School

Provost Marshal General's School
Army Air Defense School
Armor School
Army Artillery and Missile School
Army Aviation School
Army Chaplain's School
Army Chemical Corps School
Army Cold Weather & Mountain School
Army Engineer School
Army Infantry School
Army Intelligence School
Army Information School
Army Language School
Army Medical Service School
Army Medical Service Meat & Dairy Hygiene School
Army Ordnance School
Army Primary Helicopter School
Army Quartermaster School
Army Signal School
Army Strategic Intelligence School
Army Transportation School
Women's Army School
Naval Damage Control School
Naval Intelligence School
Optical & Gunnery Officer's School
Fleet Sonar & Electronics School
Naval Amphibious Training Commands (varied)
Fleet Air Defense Training Centers (varied)
Submarine School
General Line School
Naval School of Naval Justice
Marine Corps Amphibious Warfare School
Marine Corps Communications Officer's School
Army War College
Air Command & Staff School
Air War College
Air Tactical School
Air University
National War College
USAF Special Staff School
School of Aviation Medicine
Air Force Flight Training Schools (various)
Naval Air Flight Training Schools (various)

COMBAT EFFECTIVENESS
    Excellent
SPECIAL NOTES
    It is anticipated that to support future defense programs, the budget will move close to $128-billion in the next fiscal year.

UPPER VOLTA

Defense Budget	$ 6,000,000
Population	6,097,000
Manpower in the Armed Forces	2,000
Defense as % of GNP	3%

ARMY

MANPOWER
 2,000 men

GENERAL
 Organized as 2 infantry battalions, 1 armored car recon squadron, 1 paratroop company, and 1 engineer company.

PRINCIPAL EQUIPMENT
 Weapons: Conventional
  Ferret Armored Cars
  Mortars
 Aircraft: 2 Transports
  3 Light Aircraft

NAVY

None.

AIR FORCE

None.

MISCELLANEOUS DATA

DEFENSE AGREEMENTS
 Equatorial Defense Council

MAP TYPE ASSISTANCE RECEIVED FROM
 France, Israel, U.S., U.S.S.R.

INTERNAL SECURITY FORCES
 1,835 men

CONSCRIPTION LAW
 Volunteer forces

NATIONAL FLAG
 Horizontal stripes of black, white and red.

OFFICIAL LANGUAGE
 French

COMBAT EFFECTIVENESS
 Limited

SPECIAL NOTES
 Country was taken over by military in 1974.

 A peace agreement was signed with Mali in 1975, ending a long dispute over the Beli River.

URUGUAY

Defense Budget	$ 67,000,000
Population	3,100,000
Manpower in the Armed Forces	21,000
Defense as % of GNP	5.2%

ARMY

MANPOWER
    16,000 men (Reserves of 100,000)

GENERAL
    Organized into 2 armored, 5 infantry regiments, 9 cavalry squadrons, 5 artillery battalions, 6 engineer battalions.

PRINCIPAL EQUIPMENT
    <u>Weapons</u>:
        8 M-24 Tanks
        11 M-3 Scout Cars
        21 M-113 Armored Personnel Carriers
        Light Artillery

NAVY

MANPOWER
    3,000 men

PRINCIPAL EQUIPMENT
    <u>Vessels</u>:
        3 Destroyer Escorts
        2 Patrol Escorts
        1 Coastal Minesweeper
        3 Sub Chasers
        1 Minelayer
        4 Auxiliaries
    <u>Aircraft</u>:
        3 S-2 ASW Aircraft
        2 Bell 47s
        4 OH-23s
        2 L-21s

AIR FORCE

MANPOWER
    2,000 men

PRINCIPAL EQUIPMENT
    <u>Aircraft</u>:

	Fighters	6 F-80s
		6 T-33 Armed Trainers
		20 T-6 Armed Trainers
	Transports	12 C-47s
		1 DHC-2
		3 C-45s
		4 F-27s
		8 U-17s
	Helicopters	2 Bell UH-1s
		2 Hiller UH-12s

URUGUAY

MISCELLANEOUS DATA

DEFENSE AGREEMENTS
    Rio Pact
MAP TYPE ASSISTANCE RECEIVED FROM
    U.S.
INTERNAL SECURITY FORCES
    22,000 men
CONSCRIPTION LAW
    Compulsory service for 2 years.
NATIONAL FLAG
    Four blue stripes on a white background with a
golden sun in the upper left corner.
OFFICIAL LANGUAGE
    Spanish
COMBAT EFFECTIVENESS
    Limited
SPECIAL NOTES
    Country was taken over by military coup in 1973 and
has remained so ever since. Major complaints have been
made as to the handling of political prisoners (some
4,000 have been tried before tribunals) in international
circles.

Defense Budget	$ 305,000,000
Population	10,788,000
Manpower in the Armed Forces	40,500
Defense as % of GNP	3.0%

DEFENSE ESTABLISHMENT

The President, through the Minister of Defense, exercises control over the armed services. There are four independent services -- the Army, Navy, Air Force and National Guard.

ARMY

MANPOWER
 24,000 men
GENERAL
 Currently being reorganized.
PRINCIPAL EQUIPMENT
 Weapons: Est. 150 AMX-30 Tanks
             15 AMX-13s
             M-18 Tank Destroyers
             55 Armored Cars
             20 Pieces of 155 Artillery
             Light Artillery

NAVY

MANPOWER
 7,500 men (includes 3,000 Marines)
PRINCIPAL EQUIPMENT
 Vessels: 4 Submarines
             4 Destroyers
             6 Destroyer Escorts
            10 Patrol Craft
             3 Fast Patrol Boats w/Missiles
             3 Fast Patrol Boats
             5 Landing Ships
             3 Survey Ships
            12 Coast Guard Vessels (11 operated by
                National Guard)
             3 Light Transports

AIR FORCE

MANPOWER
 9,000 men
PRINCIPAL EQUIPMENT
 Aircraft: Fighter-Bombers   18 CF-5s
                                13 Mirage IIIs
                                20 F-86s
             Bombers   26 Canberras
                                16 OV-16s
                                 8 B-25s

VENEZUELA

Reconnaissance	2 Canberras
Transports	12 C-47s
	13 C-123s
	4 C-130s
	1 H.S. 748
Helicopters	4 Bell 47Gs
	16 Bell UH-1s
	20 Alouette IIIs
	4 UH-19s

BASES
    Caracas, Maracay, Barcelona, Barquisimento.

MISCELLANEOUS DATA

DEFENSE AGREEMENTS
    Rio Pact
MAP TYPE ASSISTANCE RECEIVED FROM
    U.S., W. Germany
INTERNAL SECURITY FORCES
    National Guard - 10,000
CONSCRIPTION LAW
    Compulsory service for 2 years at age 18
MILITARY SCHOOLS
    Each of the four services has a Military Academy.
NATIONAL FLAG
    Horizontal stripes of yellow, blue and red, with seven white stars in the center and the national coat of arms in the upper left.
OFFICIAL LANGUAGE
    Spanish
COMBAT EFFECTIVENESS
    Limited

Defense Budget	$ 350,000,000
Population	43,000,000
Manpower in the Armed Forces	513,000
Defense as % of GNP	15%

Since the fall of South Vietnam, the picture concerning the current status of the now unified nation has been unclear -- as a result, we provide only the best estimates on today's forces.

ARMY

MANPOWER
 500,000 men

GENERAL
 Organized into 14 divisions: 10 artillery and 4 armored regiments, 20 independent infantry regiments, 30 missile battalions.

PRINCIPAL EQUIPMENT
 <u>Weapons</u>:
  1,000 T-54/59 Tanks
  300 PT-76/Type 60 Tanks
  250+ BTR-40 Armored Personnel Carriers
  6,000+ AA Guns
  Light and Heavy Artillery (est. 800 pcs.)
 <u>Missiles</u>:
  Guideline
  Sagger AT
  Goa

NAVY

MANPOWER
 3,000 men

PRINCIPAL EQUIPMENT
 <u>Vessels</u>:
  3 Coastal Escorts
  25 Motor Gun Boats
  20 Motor Torpedo Boats
  30 Patrol Boats
  20 Landing Craft
  15 Armed Junks
 <u>Aircraft</u>: Helicopters 10 Mi-4s

AIR FORCE

MANPOWER
 10,000 men

PRINCIPAL EQUIPMENT
 <u>Aircraft</u>:
  Bombers   12 IL-28s
  Fighter-Bombers 100+ MIG-15/17s
  Interceptors   100 MIG-21s
                   30   MIG-19s
  Helicopters   15   Mi-4s
                   10   Mi-6s
  Transports   20   An-2s
                   3   An-24s
                   12   IL-14s
                   20   Li-2s

VIETNAM

Missiles: Atoll

MISCELLANEOUS DATA

DEFENSE AGREEMENTS
    Red China, U.S.S.R.
MAP TYPE ASSISTANCE RECEIVED FROM
    Red China, U.S.S.R.
INTERNAL SECURITY FORCES
    425,000 men (People's Self-Defense Force of
1.5-million).
CONSCRIPTION LAW
    Compulsory service for 3 years.
NATIONAL FLAG
    A red field with a 5-pointed gold star in the
center.
OFFICIAL LANGUAGE
    Vietnamese
COMBAT EFFECTIVENESS
    Excellent
SPECIAL NOTES
    Since the end of the war in Vietnam and due to its
rapid ending, much of the U.S. military aid to South
Vietnam was left behind. It is estimated that
facilities, piers, docks and serviceable equipment
valued at over $2-billion was left behind.
    Included in this is about 300 vessels of varying
types used in river patrol and close-in shore operations.
    Ammunition valued at over $50-million was left
behind in servicable condition.
    The majority of aircraft were flown out to other
countries and many jettisoned at sea. An estimated
300 were left behind.
    It is estimated that something in the order of 200
tanks, armored cars, and armored personnel carriers
were left, which could be brought into serviceable
condition.

YEMEN, NORTH

Defense Budget	$ 60,000,000
Population	6,670,000
Manpower in the Armed Forces	25,000
Defense as % of GNP	N.A.

ARMY

MANPOWER
    23,000 men
GENERAL
    Organized into brigades: 1 parachute, 6 infantry, 1 commando; plus 2 armored battalions, guard battalion, anand 2 artillery battalions.
PRINCIPAL EQUIPMENT
    Weapons: 30 T-43 Tanks
                35 Armored Cars
                80 Armored Personnel Carriers
                Light and Heavy Artillery

NAVY

MANPOWER
    300 men
PRINCIPAL EQUIPMENT
    Vessels: 3 Fast Patrol Boats

AIR FORCE

MANPOWER
    1,700 men
PRINCIPAL EQUIPMENT
    Aircraft: Fighter-Bombers   12 MIG-17s
                Bombers   16 IL-28s
                Transports   6 C-47s
                                   8 IL-14s
                                   3 Li-2s
                                   2 Skyvans
                Helicopters   11 Mi-4s

MISCELLANEOUS DATA

DEFENSE AGREEMENTS
    Arab League
MAP TYPE ASSISTANCE RECEIVED FROM
    U.S.S.R., Red China, Saudi Arabia, East Germany.
INTERNAL SECURITY FORCES
    20,000 men
CONSCRIPTION LAW
    Volunteer forces

NATIONAL FLAG
    Horizontal stripes of red, white and black with a
 green star in center.
OFFICIAL LANGUAGE
    Arabic
COMBAT EFFECTIVENESS
    Limited
SPECIAL NOTES
    Country under military control since 1974.

    Reports indicate that there are between 3/4,000
Soviet, 200 East German, and 200 Cuban 'advisors' in
the country.

Defense Budget $ 30,000,000
Population 1,335,000
Manpower in the Armed Forces 14,000
Defense as % of GNP 4.0%

ARMY

MANPOWER
    11,000 men
GENERAL
    Organized into 6 infantry brigades, 1 armored battalion, 1 artillery brigade, 2 communications units, 1 training battalion.
PRINCIPAL EQUIPMENT
    <u>Weapons</u>:   48 T-34/54 Tanks
                  Armored Cars
                  Light Artillery

NAVY

MANPOWER
    300 men
PRINCIPAL EQUIPMENT
    <u>Vessels</u>:   2 Sub Chasers
                 3 Minesweepers
                 3 Landing Craft

AIR FORCE

MANPOWER
    2,700 men
PRINCIPAL EQUIPMENT

<u>Aircraft</u>:	Fighters	12 MIG-21s
		12 MIG-17s
		10 MIG-15s
	Counter-Insurgency	4 BAC-167s
		8 Provosts
	Transports	4 IL-28s
		4 An-24s
		2 IL-14s
	Bombers	4 IL-28s
	Helicopters	14 Mi-4/8s
		2 Bell 47s

MISCELLANEOUS DATA

DEFENSE AGREEMENTS
    Arab League
MAP TYPE ASSISTANCE RECEIVED FROM
    U.S.S.R., Red China

YEMEN, SOUTH
(P.D.R.)

INTERNAL SECURITY FORCES
    10,000 men
NATIONAL FLAG
    Horizontal stripes of red, white and black with a blue triangle at the left containing a red star.
OFFICIAL LANGUAGE
    Arabic
COMBAT EFFECTIVENESS
    Limited
SPECIAL NOTES
    Soviet Union has become principal supplier of military aid.

Defense Budget	$ 1,300,000,000
Population	21,330,000
Manpower in the Armed Forces	225,000
Defense as % of GNP	8.5%

ARMY

MANPOWER
 185,000 men (Reserves of over 1-million)

GENERAL
 Organized into 9 infantry divisions, 1 armored division, 20 independent infantry brigades, 12 independent tank brigades, mountain and airborne units.

PRINCIPAL EQUIPMENT
 Weapons: 1,500+ Tanks (T-34/54, M-47)
  500+ M-24 Tanks
  AMX-13, PT-76 Tanks
  Light and Heavy Artillery
 Missiles: Snapper AT
  Sagger AT

NAVY

MANPOWER
 20,000 men

PRINCIPAL EQUIPMENT
 Vessels: 5 Submarines
  2 Destroyers
  10 Guided Missile Boats
  70 Torpedo Boats
  12 River Minesweepers
  4 Coastal Minesweepers
  18 Inshore Minesweepers
  34 Landing Craft
  20 Auxiliaries and Support Ships
 Missiles: Styx

AIR FORCE

MANPOWER
 20,000 men

PRINCIPAL EQUIPMENT
 Aircraft:
  Fighter-Bombers 20 Kraguj Close Support
  90 Galeb/Jastreb Light Attack
  10 F-84s
  Interceptors 100+ MIG-21s
  Reconnaissance 15 RT-33s
  25 Galeb/Jastrebs
  Transports 12 C-47s
  13 IL-14s
  6 IL-18s
  2 An-1s

YUGOSLAVIA 251

                Helicopters   35 Mi-4s
                                    24 Mi-8s
                                     5 Alouette IIIs
                                 125 Gazelles
                                  12 Whirlwinds

   <u>Missiles</u>:   Guideline
                Atoll

BASES
    Batajnica, Cerklje, Zemun, Zagreb, Ljubljana, Kotor, Titograd, Nis, Sarajevo, Pleso, Pula, Nickoic, Mostar, Sombor, Salusani, Vrsac.

MISCELLANEOUS DATA

MAP TYPE ASSISTANCE RECEIVED FROM
    U.S., U.S.S.R.
INTERNAL SECURITY FORCES
    20,000 men - 3-million in Territorial Defense Force.
CONSCRIPTION LAW
    All citizens 19 to 27 liable for service; 18 months in Army, 24 months in Navy and Air Force.
NATIONAL FLAG
    Horizontal stripes of blue, white and red with a red star outlined in gold in the center.
OFFICIAL LANGUAGE
    Serbo-Croatian
COMBAT EFFECTIVENESS
    Excellent
SPECIAL NOTES
    Yugoslavia maintains relations with the Soviets and U.S. and attempts to play a balance between the two in its own national interests.
    In 1975, a long-standing dispute with Italy over Trieste was resolved.

Defense Budget	$ 120,000,000
Population	26,640,000
Manpower in the Armed Forces	50,000
Defense as % of GNP	5.6%

ARMY

MANPOWER
   49,000 men

GENERAL
   Organized into 1 armored car regiment; 14 infantry battalions, 7 parachute battalions, 1 mechanized battalion, 4 commando battalions, support units.

PRINCIPAL EQUIPMENT
   <u>Weapons</u>:   90 AML-60 and AML-90 Armored Cars
                    30 Ferret Scout Cars
                    10 M-3 Scout Cars
                    Light Artillery

NAVY

MANPOWER
   150 men

GENERAL
   Operates as Coast Guard and River patrol.

PRINCIPAL EQUIPMENT
   <u>Vessels</u>:   7 River Gunboats
                    1 Patrol Boat
                    1 River Boat

AIR FORCE

MANPOWER
   850 men

PRINCIPAL EQUIPMENT
   <u>Aircraft</u>:
         Counter-Insurgency   17 MB326 Armed Trainers
                                6 AT-6 Armed Trainers
                               11 T-28 Armed Trainers
         Fighter-Bombers   17 Mirage Vs
         Transports   6 C-130s
                                8 C-47s
                                4 C-54s
         Helicopters   20 Alouette II/IIIs
                                7 Pumas

MISCELLANEOUS DATA

MAP TYPE ASSISTANCE RECEIVED FROM
   U.S., U.S.S.R., Israel, Italy, Belgium, Nigeria.
INTERNAL SECURITY FORCES
   15,000 men

ZAIRE

CONSCRIPTION LAW
    Volunteer forces
NATIONAL FLAG
    A green field with yellow circle surrounding a
 red torch.
OFFICIAL LANGUAGE
    French
COMBAT EFFECTIVENESS
    Limited
SPECIAL NOTES
    Zaire is the former Republic of the Congo (Kinshasa).

Defense Budget $ 80,000,000
Population 4,558,470
Manpower in the Armed Forces 5,800
Defense as % of GNP 3.1%

DEFENSE ESTABLISHMENT

Supreme authority over the armed forces is vested in the President, who is also empowered to determine the operational use of the armed forces. A Secretary of Defense in the president's office acts as a coordinator between the Defense Council and the military commanders. The Armed Forces have no general staff.

ARMY

MANPOWER
  5,000 men (Reserves of 2,000)
GENERAL
  The army's mission is two-fold: to assist the police in maintaining internal security; and, defense of borders against foreign incursion.
  Organized into 4 infantry battalions, 1 recon unit, 2 artillery batteries, 1 SAM battery, and engineer and communications squadrons.
PRINCIPAL EQUIPMENT
  Weapons: Limited Artillery
           Armored Cars
  Missiles: Rapier

NAVY

None.

AIR FORCE

MANPOWER
  800
PRINCIPAL EQUIPMENT
  Aircraft: Light Tactical   4 SOKO Jastrebs
                             8 Marchetti 260s
                            18 Aeromacchi 326s
            Transports   10 Do-28ds
                            10 C-47s
                             5 DH-2s
                             5 DH-4s
                             5 DH-5s
            Helicopters   13 Alouette II/IIIs
                            25 Bell 205s
                             7 Bell 47Gs
BASES
  Lusaka, Mbala, Mumbwa, Siluwe, Livingstone, Ndola, Chipata, Kasama, Mongu.

ZAMBIA

MISCELLANEOUS DATA

DEFENSE AGREEMENTS
    U.K.
MAP TYPE ASSISTANCE RECEIVED FROM
    Italy, U.K., Yugoslavia
CONSCRIPTION LAW
    Volunteer forces
MILITARY SCHOOLS
    School of Military Training
NATIONAL FLAG
    Green field with swatch in the lower right hand corner of red, black and orange vertical stripes topped by an orange flying eagle.
OFFICIAL LANGUAGE
    English
COMBAT EFFECTIVENESS
    Limited

THE FOLLOWING COUNTRIES EITHER HAVE NO ARMED FORCES PER SE, OR UTILIZE THEIR INTERNAL SECURITY FORCES FOR ALL SECURITY MEASURES:

Barbados	Monaco
Brunei	Namibia
Cape Verde Islands	Nauru
Comoro Islands	Panama
Equatorial Guinea	Papua New Guinea
Fiji	Sao Tome & Principe
Grenada	Surinam
Guinea-Bissau	Swaziland
Guyana	Tonga
Liechtenstein	Vatican City State
Maldives	Western Samoa
Mauritius	

APPENDIXES

I	Key Defense Agreements and Treaties
II	Defense Treaties of the United States
III	Munitions Production Capabilities of Each Nation
IV	Nuclear Weapons Potential of All Countries
V	Capabilities for Military Attacks from Space
VI	U.S. Third World Security Assistance Funding
VII	The Critical Middle East Situation
VIII	Major Middle East Procurements Since Third Edition
IX	Military Posture -- U.S. versus U.S.S.R.
X	Official Name and Location of Defense Headquarters

KEY DEFENSE AGREEMENTS AND TREATIES

NORTH ATLANTIC TREATY ORGANIZATION -- NATO
Canada, Iceland, Belgium, Denmark, France, Federal Republic of Germany, Greece, Italy, Luxembourg, Netherlands, Norway, Portugal, Turkey, United Kingdom, United States.

ARAB LEAGUE
Algeria, Bahrain, Egypt, Iraq, Libya, Jordan, Kuwait, Lebanon, Mauritania, Morocco, Oman, Qatar, Saudi Arabia, Somalia, Sudan, Syria, Tunisia, United Arab Emirates, Yemen Arab Republic, Yemen People's Democratic Republic.

CENTRAL TREATY ORGANIZATION -- CENTO
Iran, Pakistan, Turkey, United Kingdom (U.S. Observer status)

ORGANIZATION OF AFRICAN UNITY -- OAU
Algeria, Benin, Botswana, Burundi, Cameroon, Cape Verde, Central African Republic, Chad, Comoro Islands, Congo, Egypt, Equatorial Guinea, Ethiopia, Gabon, Gambia, Ghana, Guinea, Guinea-Bissau, Ivory Coast Kenya, Lesotho, Liberia, Libya, Malagasy, Malawi, Mali, Mauritania, Mauritius, Morocco, Mozambique, Niger, Nigeria, Rwanda, Sao Tome and Principe, Senegal, Sierra Leone, Somalia, Sudan, Swaziland, Tanzania, Toga, Tunisia, Uganda, Upper Volta, Zaire, Zambia.

ORGANIZATION OF AMERICAN STATES -- OAS
Argentina, Barbados, Bolivia, Brazil, Chile, Colombia, Costa Rica, Dominican Republic, Ecuador, El Salvador, Guatemala, Haiti, Honduras, Jamaica, Mexico, Nicaragua, Panama, Paraguay, Peru, Trinidad and Tobago, United States, Uruguay, Venezuela.

WARSAW TREATY ORGANIZATION -- WTO
Bulgaria, Czechoslovakia, German Democratic Republic, Hungary, Romania, Poland, Union of Soviet Socialist Republics.

ARAB LEAGUE UNIFIED COMMAND
Algeria, Libya, Morocco, Sudan, United Arab Republic.

RIO TREATY
Honduras, Mexico, Guatemala, El Salvador, Nicaragua, Haiti, Dominican Republic, Costa Rica, Panama, Venezuela, Ecuador, Colombia, Peru, Bolivia, Paraguay, Brazil, Chile, Argentina, Uruguay, United States.

MUTUAL DEFENSE AGREEMENTS
United States with Australia, New Zealand, Japan, Philippines, Taiwan, South Korea.

UNION AFRICANE ET MALGACHE
Cameroon, Central African Republic, Chad, Congo, Benin, Gabon, Ivory Coast, Mauritania, Niger, Rwanda, Senegal, Toga, Upper Volta.

APPENDIX II

DEFENSE TREATIES

Treaty with	NATO	RIO	SEATO	U.S.-Philippines	U.S.-Japan Security	U.S.-Rep. of Korea	U.S.-Rep. of China
Belgium	X						
Canada	X						
Denmark	X						
France	X						
W. Germany	X						
Greece	X						
Iceland	X						
Italy	X						
Luxembourg	X						
Netherlands	X						
Portugal	X						
Norway	X						
Turkey	X						
U.K.	X		X				
U.S.	X	X	X	X	X	X	X
Argentina		X					
Bolivia		X					
Brazil		X					
Chile		X					
Colombia		X					
Costa Rica		X					
Cuba							
Dominican Rep.		X					
Equador		X					
El Salvador		X					
Guatemala		X					
Haiti		X					
Honduras		X					
Mexico		X					
Nicaragua		X					
Panama		X					
Paraguay		X					
Peru		X					
Uruguay		X					
Venezuela		X					
Australia			X				
New Zealand			X				
Pakistan			X				
Philippines			X	X			
Thailand			X				
Japan					X		
Rep/Korea						X	
Rep/China							X

```
NATO    April 4, 1949     Philippines Mutual Defense - Aug. 30, 1951
RIO     Sept. 2, 1947     Japanese Security          - Jan. 19, 1960
SEATO   Sept. 8, 1954     China Treaty               - Dec. 2, 1954
```

MUNITIONS PRODUCTION CAPABILITIES OF EACH NATION

Country	No Known Capability	Manufacture of Small Arms/Ammo.	Manufacture of Heavy Weapons/ Aircraft/Tanks
Afghanistan		X	
Albania		X	
Algeria		X	
Andorra			
Argentina		X	X
Australia		X	X
Austria		X	X
Belgium		X	X
Bhutan			
Bolivia		X	
Brazil		X	X
Bulgaria		X	X
Burma		X	
Burundi		X	
Cambodia		X	
Cameroon		X	
Canada		X	X
Central African Republic	X		
Chad	X		
Ceylon		X	
Chile		X	X
China (Communist)		X	X
China (Nationalist)		X	X
Colombia		X	
Congo-Kinshasa		X	
Costa Rica		X	
Cuba		X	X
Cyprus		X	
Czechoslovakia		X	X
Dahomey		X	
Denmark		X	X
Dominican Republic		X	
East Germany		X	X
Ecuador		X	
El Salvador		X	
Ethiopia		X	
Finland		X	
France		X	X
Gabon		X	
Gambia			
Ghana	X	X	

(continued)

APPENDIX III

Country	No Known Capability	Manufacture of Small Arms/Ammo.	Manufacture of Heavy Weapons/ Aircraft/Tanks
Greece		X	X
Guatemala		X	
Guinea		X	
Haiti		X	
Honduras		X	
Hungary		X	X
Iceland	X		
India		X	X
Indonesia		X	
Iran		X	
Iraq		X	
Irish Republic		X	
Israel		X	X
Italy		X	X
Ivory Coast		X	
Jamaica		X	
Japan		X	X
Jordan		X	
Kenya		X	
Korea (North)		X	
Korea (South)		X	
Kuwait	X		
Laos		X	
Lebanon		X	
Liberia		X	
Libya	X		
Liechtenstein	X		
Luxembourg	X		
Madagascar	X		
Malawi	X		
Malaysia		X	
Mali		X	
Malta	X		
Mauritania	X		
Mexico		X	X
Monaco	X		
Mongolia		X	
Morocco		X	
Muscat & Oman	X		
Nepal		X	
Netherlands		X	X
New Zealand		X	X
Nicaragua		X	
Niger	X		
Nigeria		X	
Norway		X	X

(continued)

Country	No Known Capability	Manufacture of Small Arms/Ammo.	Manufacture of Heavy Weapons/ Aircraft/Tanks
Pakistan		X	X
Panama		X	
Paraguay		X	
Persian Gulf States		X	
Peru		X	
Philippines		X	X
Poland		X	X
Portugal		X	X
Rhodesia		X	
Rumania		X	X
Rwanda	X		
San Marino	X		
Saudi Arabia		X	
Senegal		X	
Sierra Leone		X	
Singapore		X	
Somalia		X	
South Africa		X	X
Spain		X	X
Sudan		X	
Sweden		X	X
Switzerland		X	X
Syria		X	
Tanzania		X	
Thailand		X	X
Toga		X	
Tibet	X		
Trinidad & Tobago		X	
Tunisia		X	
Turkey		X	X
Uganda		X	
U.S.S.R.		X	X
United Arab Republic		X	X
United Kingdom		X	X
United States		X	X
Upper Volta		X	
Uruguay		X	X
Vatican City	X		
Venezuela		X	X
Vietnam (South)		X	
Vietnam (North)		X	
West Germany		X	X
Western Samoa	X		
Yemen		X	
Yugoslavia		X	X
Zambia		X	

APPENDIX IV

NUCLEAR WEAPONS POTENTIALS OF ALL COUNTRIES

A. IMMEDIATE
Capability to use nuclear weapons today:

    United States
    U.S.S.R.
    Communist China
    India
    United Kingdom
    France
    Israel

B. IMPENDING
Capability to use nuclear weapons within 3 years:

    Canada   Spain
    Italy   Sweden
    Japan   Switzerland
    South Africa Taiwan

C. FUTURE
Capability to use nuclear weapons within 4 to 6 years:

    Argentina   Denmark
    Austria   East Germany
    Belgium   Netherlands
    Brazil   Norway
    Czechoslovakia Poland
                   South Korea

Capability to use nuclear weapons within 7 to 10 years:

    Egypt   Portugal
    Finland   Rumania
    Iran   Turkey
    Mexico   Yugoslavia
    Pakistan

D. U.S. vs SOVIET INTERCONTINENTAL STRATEGIC NUCLEAR FORCES

	U.S.	U.S.S.R.
ICBM Launchers	1,054	1,590
SLBM Launchers	656	760
Intercontinental Bombers	498	860
Sub-Launched Cruise Missiles	0	314
	2,208	3,524

CAPABILITIES FOR MILITARY ATTACKS FROM SPACE

A. IMMEDIATE

    Capability to launch weapons vehicles from the ground into space and return to earth:

        United States
        U.S.S.R.
        United Kingdom
        France

B. FUTURE

    Capability to launch weapons vehicles from the ground into space and return to earth in next five years:

        Communist China
        Israel
        West Germany

CAPABILITIES FOR SPACE BASED WEAPONS SYSTEMS

A. IMMEDIATE

    Capability to launch a military attack with a weapon based in space after a long period when weapon system was placed into orbit:

        United States
        U.S.S.R.

B. FUTURE

    Capability to launch a military attack with a space based weapon within the next five years:

        France
        U.K.

CAPABILITY OF GROUND DEFENSE SYSTEM TO ATTACK SPACE BASED WEAPON SYSTEMS

The technology currently exists within both the United States and U.S.S.R. to attack a space-based weapons system.

APPENDIX VI

U.S. THIRD WORLD SECURITY ASSISTANCE FUNDING, FY 1955-1975
(millions of dollars)

COUNTRY:

Country	Amount
Argentina	133
Austria	143
Bolivia	19
Brazil	301
Burma	65
Cambodia	1,031
Chile	92
Colombia	78
Costa Rica	2
Dahomey	1
Dominican Republic	19
Ecuador	28
El Salvador	5
Ethiopia	148
Guatemala	28
Haiti	2
Honduras	6
India	112
Indonesia	96
Iran	2,521
Iraq	55
Israel	2,515
Jamaica	1
Jordan	309
Kuwait	4
Laos	242
Lebanon	19
Liberia	6
Libya	33
Malaysia	36
Mali	2
Mexico	12
Morocco	60
Nepal	2
Nicaragua	8
Oman	1
Pakistan	601
Panama	5
Paraguay	6
Peru	96
Philippines	322
Saudi Arabia	357
Senegal	2
Singapore	12
South Africa	3
Spain	738
Sri Lanka	3
Thailand	414
Tunisia	35
Uruguay	34
Venezuela	135
Yemen (North)	2
Zaire	38
	10,873-millions

THE CRITICAL MIDDLE EAST SITUATION

The Middle East remains as the world's most sensitive region and the following charts indicate the ratio of military power between Israel and the Arab states:

1976

Balance of Power Arab States vs Israel

	Confrontation area - Arab States[1]	Arab states plus anticipated contribution by states outside confrontation Area[2]
Combat aircraft	2.8 to 1	3 to 1
Tanks	2.7 to 1	3 to 1
Artillery	6 to 1	9 to 1
Armed forces (divisions)	4 to 1	5 to 1
SAM batteries	10 to 1	12 to 1

[1] Egypt, Syria and Jordan.

[2] Egypt, Syria, Jordan, Iraq, Saudi Arabia, Kuwait, Libya, Algeria, Morocco, Sudan and Tunisia.

1980

Force Levels Arab States Are Anticipated to Contribute in Future War With Israel

Eastern Front - Syria, Jordan, Iraq, Saudi Arabia, Kuwait

Divisions	20
Combat Aircraft	1,000
Tanks	5,400
Armored personnel carriers	5,000
Artillery pieces	3,000
SAM batteries	150

Western Front - Egypt, Libya, Algeria, Morocco, Sudan, Tunisia

Divisions	15
Combat Aircraft	1,000
Tanks	3,500
Armored Personnel carriers	3,850
Artillery pieces	2,800
SAM batteries	250

MAJOR MIDDLE EAST PROCUREMENTS SINCE THIRD EDITION

Abu Dhabi
 32 Mirage V fighter-bombers costing $230,000,000.
 18 Mirage III-E fighter-bombers costing $125,000,000.

Iraq
 40 MIG-23 fighters - no dollar value known.
 40 French Alouette III helicopters.

Jordan
 24 F-5 fighters from Iran.
 36 F-5E fighter-bombers costing $200,000,000+.

Kuwait
 36 A-4 Skyhawk fighter-bombers costing $250,000,000.
 18 Jaguar fighter-bombers costing $63,000,000.

Libya (as part of $2-billion package)
 40 Mirage F-1 fighters
 12 Tu-22 bombers
 29 MIG-23 fighters

Saudi Arabia
 38 Mirage III-E fighter bombers (both costing
 450 AMX-10/30 tanks, Crotale missiles $870,000,000)
 90 F-5E fighter-bombers costing $1,095,000,000.
 200 Bell AH-1J Sea Cobra helicopters (the first of 400 to be delivered).

Syria
 130 MIG-21 fighter-bombers - no dollar value known.
 60 MIG-23 fighters - no dollar value known.
 15-40 Super Frelon helicopters - no dollar value known.

Egypt
 20 Mirage F-1 fighters costing $315,000,000 (paid for by Kuwait)
 38 Mirage IIIs paid for by Saudi Arabia.
 60 Mirages to be ordered by Egypt in next 2 years.
 25 MIG-23 fighters.
 24 Westland Commando troop-transport helicopters.
 24 SA-842 Gazelle helicopters with MBB At missiles.
 44 Mirage F-1 fighters

  Since 1973, the Arab States have received or have on order military equipment with a total sales value of over $15-billion. Thus, the Middle East build-up will go down on record as the highest in history for comprehensive purchases by other than the NATO and Warsaw Pact nations.

MILITARY POSTURE -- U.S. VERSUS U.S.S.R.

	U.S.	U.S.S.R.
I. Strategic Offense Forces		
ICBM Launchers	1,054	1,590
SLBM Launchers	656	800
Intercontinental Bombers	498	140
Sub-launched Cruise Missiles	0	314
	2,208	2,844
II. Strategic Defense Forces		
Surface-to-Air Missiles (launcher (launchers)	0	12,000
Air Defense Interceptor Aircraft	333	546
III. Principal Ground Force Weapons		
Tanks	9,000	40,000
Armored personnel carriers and other combat vehicles	22,000	30/40,000
Artillery peices	6,000	15/20,000
Heavy mortars	3,000	5/10,000
Helicopters	9,000	2,000
Tactical Aircraft	4,100	5,700
IV. Military Manpower		
Active Military Forces	2.1-million	4.4-million
Reserves	1.8-million	6.8=million
	3.9-million	11.2-million

APPENDIX X

OFFICIAL NAME AND LOCATION OF DEFENSE HEADQUARTERS

Afghanistan
Ministry of Defense
Kabul

Albania
Ministry of Defense
Tirana

Algeria
Ministry of Defense
Algiers

Angola
Ministry of Defense
Luanda

Argentina
Ministerio De Guerra
Buenos Aires

Australia
Department of Defense
Canberra

Austria
Ministry of National Defense
Vienna

Bahrain
Ministry of Defense
Manama

Bangladesh
Ministry of Defense
Dacca

Belgium
Ministere De La Defense Nationale
2 rue la Loi
Bruxelles 1

Benin (Dahomey)
Ministry of Defense
Porto Novo

Bhutan
Ministry of Defense
Thimpu

Bolivia
Ministerio De Defensa
La Paz

Botswana
Ministry of Defense
Gaborone

Brazil
Ministere De Defensa
Rio de Janiero

Brunei
Ministry of Defense
Bandar Seri Begawan

Bulgaria
Ministere De La Defense Nationale
Sofia

Burma
Ministry of Defense
Rangoon

Burundi
Ministry of Defense
Bujumbura

Cambodia
Ministere De La Defense
Phnom Penh

Cameroon
Ministry of Defense
Yaounde

Canada
Department of National Defense
Ottawa

Central African Republic
Ministere De Defense
Bangui

Chad
Ministere De Defense
N'Djamena

Chile
Ministerio De Defensa Nacional
Santiago

China, Rep. of
Ministry of Defense
Peking

Colombia
Ministerio De Guerra
Bogata

APPENDIX X

Congo, Rep. of
Ministere De Defense
Brazzaville

Costa Rica
Ministerio De La Defensa
San Jose

Cuba
Ministerio De Defensa
Havana

Cyprus
Ministry of Defense
Nicosia

Czechoslovakia
Ministerstvo Narodni Obrany
Prague

Denmark
Ministry of Defense
Copenhagen

Dominican Republic
Ministerio De Defensa
Santo Domingo

Ecuador
Ministerio De Defense Nacional
Quito

Egypt
Ministere De La Guerre
Cairo

El Salvador
Ministerio De Defensa
San Salvador

Ethiopia
Defense Ministry
Addis Ababa

Finland
Ministry of Defense
Helsinki

France
Secretariat General De La Defense Nationale
51, Bd Latour-Maubourg
Paris 7e

Gabon
Ministere De Defense
Libreville

Gambia
Ministry of Defense
Banjul

Germany, Fed. Rep.
Bundesverteidigungsrat
Koblenzer Str. 141
Bonn

German, Dem. Rep.
Defense Ministry
E. Berlin

Ghana
Ministry of Defense
Accra

Greece
Ministry of Defense
Athens

Guatemala
Ministere De Defensa
Guatemal City

Guinea
Ministere De Defensa
Conakry

Haiti
Ministere De Defensa
Port-Au-Prince

Honduras
Ministere De Defensa
Tegucigalpa

Hungary
Ministry of Defense
Dob-u 75-81
Budapest VI

Iceland
Ministry of Defense
Reykjavik

India
The Defense Ministry
New Delhi

APPENDIX X 273

<u>Indonesia</u>
<u>Ministry</u> of Defense
Djakarta

<u>Iran</u>
<u>Ministry</u> of War
Teheran

<u>Iraq</u>
<u>Ministry</u> of Defense
Baghdad

<u>Ireland</u>
<u>Ministry</u> of Defense
Dublin

<u>Israel</u>
<u>Ministry</u> of Defense
Tel-Aviv

<u>Italy</u>
Capo Delle Forze Armate Dello Stato
Via XX,
Settembre, Roma

<u>Ivory Coast, Rep.</u>
Ministere De Defense
Abidjan

<u>Jamaica</u>
Defense Ministry
Kingston

<u>Japan</u>
Kokubo Kaigi
Tokyo

<u>Jordan</u>
Ministry of Defense
Amman

<u>Kenya</u>
Ministry of Defense
Nairobi

<u>Korea (North)</u>
Ministry of Defense
Pyong-Yang

<u>Korea,(South)</u>
Defense Ministry
Seoul

Kuwait
Security Department,
Government of Kuwait
Kuwait City

Laos
Ministry of Defense
Vientiane

Lebanon
Ministere De La Defense Nationale
Beirut

Lesotho
Ministry of Defense
Maseru

Liberia
Ministry of Defense
Monrovia

Libya
Ministry of Defense
Tripoli

Madagascar
Ministry of Defense
Tananarive

Malawi
Ministry of Defense
Lilongwe

Malaysia
Defense Ministry
Kuala Lumpur

Mali
Ministere De Defense
Bamako

Mauritania
Ministry of Defense
Nouakchott

Mexico
Ministerio De La Defensa
Mexico City

Mongolia
Ministry of Defense
Ulan Bator

APPENDIX X 275

<u>Morocco</u>
Ministry of Defense
Rabat

<u>Mozambique</u>
Ministry of Defense
Lourenco-Marques

<u>Nepal</u>
Ministry of Defense
Kathmandu

<u>Netherlands</u>
Ministry of Defense
Plein 4, s'Gravehhage

<u>New Zealand</u>
Ministry of Defense
Wellington

<u>Nicaragua</u>
Ministerio De Defensa
Managua

<u>Niger</u>
Ministere De Defense
Niamey

<u>Nigeria</u>
Ministry of Defense
Lagos

<u>Norway</u>
Ministry of Defense
Oslo

<u>Oman</u>
Defense Ministry
Muscat

<u>Pakistan</u>
Ministry of Defense
Islamabad

<u>Paraguay</u>
Ministerio De Defensa Nacional
Asuncion

<u>Peru</u>
Ministerio De Defensa Nacional
Miraflores

<u>Philippines</u>
Ministry of National Defense
Manila

Poland
Ministerstwo Obrony Narodowe
Warszawa

Portugal
Ministry of Defense
Lisbon

Qatar
Defense Department
Doha

Rhodesia
Ministry of Defense
Salisbury

Rumania
Ministere Des Forces Armees
Bucharest

Rwanda
Ministry of Defense
Kigali

Saudi Arabia
Ministry of Defense
Riyadh

Senegal
Ministere De La Defense Et De La Securite
Dakar

Sierre Leone
Ministry of Defense
Freetown

Singapore
Ministry of Defense
Singapore

Somali
Ministere De Defense
Mogadishu

South Africa
Department of Defense
Pretoria

Spain
Ministerio Del Defense
Plaza de la Moncioa
Madrid

APPENDIX X 277

<u>Sri Lanka</u>
Defense Ministry
Colombo

<u>Sudan</u>
Ministry of Defense
Khartoum

<u>Sweden</u>
Ministry of Defense
Stockholm

<u>Switzerland</u>
Eidgenossisches Militardepartement
Departement Militarire
Federal
Bundeshaus Ost, Bern

<u>Syria</u>
Ministere De La Defense Nationale
Damascus

<u>Taiwan</u>
Ministry of Defense
Taipei

<u>Tanzania</u>
Ministry of Defense
Dar es Salaam

<u>Thailand</u>
Ministry of Defense
Bangkok

<u>Togo</u>
Ministry of Defense
Lome

<u>Trinidad and Tobago</u>
Defense Department
Port-of-Spain

<u>Tunisia</u>
Secretariat D'Etat A La Defense Nationale
Tunis

<u>Turkey</u>
Ministry of National Defense
Ankara

<u>Uganda</u>
Ministry of Defense
Kampala

U.S.S.R.
Ministerstvo Oborony Soyuza SSR
Moscow

United Arab Emirates
Defense Ministry
Abu Dhabi

United Kingdom
Ministry of Defense
Storey's Gate
London, S.W. 1

United States
Department of Defense
Washington, D.C.

Upper Volta
Ministere De Defense
Ouagadougou

Uruguay
Ministerio De La Defensa Nacional
Montevideo

Venezuela
Ministerio De La Defensa
Caracas

Vietnam
Ministry of Defense
Hanoi

Yemen Arab Republic
Ministry of Defense
Sana'a

Yemen, PDR
Ministry of Defense
Aden

Yugoslovia
Secretariat E'Etat Aux Affairs
 De La Defense Nationale
Kenza Milosa 29, B.P. 740

Zaire
Defense Ministry
Kinshasa

Zambia
Ministry of Defense
Lusaka

ABOUT THE EDITOR

ROBERT C. SELLERS is president of a management consulting firm that specializes in long-range planning studies for industry and government.

He has been editor of the three previous editions of Armed Forces of the World. Additionally, he was contributing editor for military affairs for the 1970 and 1971 editions of The New York Times Almanac.

He has contributed to numerous magazines and publications in the aerospace and defense fields.

RELATED TITLES
Published by
Praeger Special Studies

CURRENT ISSUES IN U.S. DEFENSE POLICY
    Center for Defense Information
    edited by David T. Johnson and
    Barry R. Schneider

THE ESTIMATION OF SOVIET DEFENSE EXPENDITURES, 1955-75:
An Unconventional Approach
    William T. Lee

*NATIONS IN ARMS: The Theory and Practice of Territorial
 Defense
    Adam Roberts

SOVIET NAVAL DEVELOPMENTS: Capability and Context
    edited by Michael MccGwire

SOVIET NAVAL INFLUENCE: Domestic and Foreign Dimensions
    edited by Michael MccGwire
    and John McDonnell

SOVIET NAVAL POLICY: Objectives and Constraints
    edited by Michael MccGwire,
    Ken Booth, and John McDonnell

THE ECONOMICS OF PEACETIME DEFENSE
    Murray L. Weidenbaum

---

*Available for sale in the United States and
the Philippines only

Ref.
UA
15
R43
4th ed.
1977

1. Ref.
2. STACKS

MAY 9 1979